THE AGE OF ABSOLUTISM

IS VOLUME

79

OF THE

Twentieth Century Encyclopedia of Catholicism

UNDER SECTION

VII

THE HISTORY OF THE CHURCH

IT IS ALSO THE

114TH

VOLUME IN ORDER OF PUBLICATION

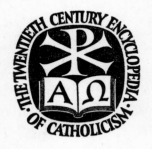

Edited by HENRI DANIEL-ROPS of the Académie Française

THE AGE OF ABSOLUTISM

By MAURICE BRAURE

HAWTHORN BOOKS · PUBLISHERS · *New York*

First Edition, December, 1963

NIHIL OBSTAT

Daniel Duivesteijn, S.T.D.

   Censor Deputatus

IMPRIMATUR

✚ Georgius L. Craven

   Episcopus Sebastopolis, Vicarius Generalis

Westmonasterii, die XXXI OCTOBRIS MCMLXIII

H-9519

CONTENTS

PART I

CATHOLIC EXPANSION IN A DIVIDED CHRISTENDOM

The history of the Church in the first half of the seventeenth century offers a striking contrast. The unhappy division which Protestantism had just caused was accompanied by a splendid flowering of the Catholic world. At the end of this period the trial of strength in the Thirty Years War ended in a balance of power, showing the division even more clearly, but the peril had produced Catholics of a new stamp; heresy had provoked more fruitful studies and wonderful reforms had given fresh life to that social nature and the missionary spirit which are essential to Christianity.

It would be a mistake to imagine that this expansion came as a result of the Reformation, or that it was inspired by it, as normally revivals and advances of this kind occur at intervals in the history of the Church, a living community. As a society of human beings, she is exposed to danger, to somnolence, to lapses, but she has always found within herself clear minds and ardent hearts to lead her forward to her destiny without any break in her magnificent continuity. And, once her divine guidance is admitted, it can be assumed that, in her darkest hours, she receives the extra grace and enlightenment that she needs. The great strides forward studied here are possibly the more striking because they follow a particularly long and troubled period and remedied great abuses.

On the other hand, the importance of the Reformation in the progress of the Church must not be denied for it was the warning shot which gave urgency to the reform already begun. Then, when it became obvious that material forces alone would not decide the conflict, recourse to spiritual values became more necessary than ever. In the other camp, also, men had died for their faith, had displayed eminent virtues and an anxious search for truth. All these were matters which could not fail to inspire in noble hearts a burning desire for that perfection which would bring back the separated brethren. Indeed, although the period was one of intolerance in general, and although political considerations loomed large, there still remained men who remembered that of the three theological virtues the greatest is charity. They were few in number, no doubt, but it was to them that the future belonged.

CHAPTER I

THE ROMAN CHURCH AND THE NATIONS, 1600–1650

Owing to the fact that the effect of the Catholic revival in France was felt particularly in the first half of the seventeenth century, there is a tendency to forget all that the previous century had contributed, in Spain and especially in Italy, towards fruitful spirituality and great achievements. But it must be recognized that, even in those countries where the unity of the faith had been maintained or re-established, politics or worldly interests were opposed to harmonious development.

Even Rome itself is an instance of this. The application of the decrees of the Council of Trent, and the measures taken by energetic popes, had practically freed the papacy from faction so that it presided with greater authority over the progress of Catholic restoration. On the other hand, the cares of a head of State prevented the pontiff from devoting himself to his religious magistracy to the full extent necessary. The splendours which the Eternal City then displayed, were, from this point of view, dearly bought.

At this time, the internal and external policies of the European States presented very grave problems to the head of the Church. In the international field, politics and religion were indeed closely associated, and inside the Catholic States their governments were showing a disturbing tendency to keep control of the clergy, thus moving towards national Churches.

To give a brief idea of the cleavage caused by the Reformation, it can be said that, ignoring isolated groups and regions where it is difficult to decide the majority, almost the whole of Northern Europe was Protestant on the eve of the Thirty Years War: England and Scotland, all Scandinavia, the United Provinces of the Netherlands, all the North and centre of Germany, Prussia, Courland, a large part of South Germany and six out of the thirteen Swiss Cantons. In Bohemia, Moravia and Hungary, Protestantism was preponderant. On the other hand, there was a large Catholic majority in the Rhine-Westphalia region, in part of the country of Main, of Bavaria, Austria and Poland. Ireland was faithful to Rome, but was persecuted and isolated. The compact Catholic body consisted of France, the Iberian Peninsula and the Spanish Netherlands, and Italy. Outside Europe, there must be added to the Catholic world, Central and South America, with the exception of the Dutch settlers in Brazil. It must not be forgotten that, in North America, English colonization was beginning, while the Spaniards and French were also interested in those regions. The other continents, to which missionaries were devoting themselves, did not play any immediate part in the politico-religious problem here under consideration.

If the Protestant countries were divided between Anglicanism, Lutheranism, Calvinism and sects of minor importance, cohesion of the Catholic world was far from being perfect, and all the large countries, which might have made themselves champions of the Church, were suffering from some serious defect. In Spain, for instance, weakened in many respects, the great obstacle to its playing a decisive rôle was the hostility shown to it by Savoy, the Venetian Republic, the Grand Duchy of Tuscany, its possessions in Naples and Milan and its fortified posts in Tuscany. The policy of the king of Spain was generally supported, it is true, by the emperor, also a

Hapsburg, but the Empire too was particularly weakened by the Reformation, by the threat from Turkey and by the short-sighted policy of the emperors who came to the throne at this period.

France, the eldest daughter of the Church, was still treating the wounds received in the Wars of Religion. The Edict of Nantes (1598) had indeed brought peace internally but it had left the Protestant minority with a solid organization. Further-more, her age-old rivalry with the House of Austria was the major obstacle to the forming of a Catholic bloc. All the same, France was the most united country with the largest popula-tion and it was to her that Clement VIII seemed inclined to turn at the beginning of the century.

Clement VIII (1592-1605) held Henri IV in esteem and helped him as arbitrator at the Peace of Vervins (1598). He also assisted him in making peace with the duke of Savoy (Treaty of Lyons, 1601). Clement was devout and hard work-ing; he was also fortunate enough to be served by remarkably intelligent cardinals, such as the Oratorian, Baronius; the Jesuits, Bellarmine and Tolet; by the two Frenchmen, d'Ossat and Du Perron, who exerted an influence favourable to France. The pope's family, the Aldobrandini, of whom one was a cardinal, did likewise. Against them were the Farnese family, supporters of Spain, and this unfortunately led to a renewal of the era of factions.

In the elections of Leo XI, who was pope for only twenty-six days, and of Paul V (1605-21), a Borghese, Spanish opposi-tion was shown by a veto against a candidate considered undesirable by the government of Philip III. This was the beginning of a practice always condemned by the curia, but which was to be used until the beginning of this century, by the emperor and the kings of France and Spain in turn.

Strangely enough, these first encroachments on the freedom of the conclave may have helped to put on the throne of St Peter, in the person of Paul V, a legal specialist, who was particularly anxious to have the laws of the Church respected. His pontificate was marked by the serious troubles he had with those States which were seeking to obtain greater independence from Rome. This was notably the case with Venice, in a long struggle, during which, for the last time in history, the whole of a territory was laid under an interdict. The republic resisted for a long time; its cause was upheld by a Servite friar, Fr Paolo Sarpi, who placed all the resources of a lively intelligence at the service of theories akin to those of the Reformation. It needed the conciliatory efforts of both France and Spain to re-establish peace.

It was with the Reformation itself that the pope had the greatest difficulties, first of all in England. At the beginning of the century, Catholics in that country were refusing in general to take the oath of supremacy recognizing the sovereign power of the king in matters both spiritual and temporal. After the Gunpowder Plot, in 1605, which may possibly have been an invention by the government to compromise the Catholics, a new form of oath, that of allegiance, was enforced on them. As the emphasis therein was put on obedience to the sovereign in temporal matters, this seemed acceptable to a number among them. Hence there arose a division among the English Catholics, but this did not last long, as the pope condemned the oath of allegiance, first in the autumn of 1606 and again in 1607.

At this very moment, the situation became very serious in Germany, where the religious conflict had inevitably become more urgent. Matters were moving towards what was to become the Thirty Years War of which Paul V saw the beginning, for he died some months after the battle of the White Mountain (1620)—a Catholic victory which was his final joy. He left behind him the reputation of a pontiff anxious to develop the Christian life, while promoting the sciences and the arts. Rome is indebted to him for most of its magnificent buildings, and it was he who had the basilica of St. Peter's completed, as a proud inscription on its façade still reminds us. It also reminds us that he loved ostentation more perhaps than he should have done, and he is sometimes reproached for excessive generosity towards his family.

His successor, Gregory XV (1621–3), suffered from poor health and entrusted many important matters to his nephew, Cardinal Ludovisi. This short pontificate is remarkable for a great success in the political field. The Holy See, indeed, was not unconnected with the transfer of the Palatine Electorate to Duke Maximilian of Bavaria, which gave a majority to the Catholics in the electoral college. This pontificate also is noteworthy for its constitution on papal elections (1621), still in force in its essentials at the present time, which freed these elections to a large extent from outside influence and in particular, at that period, from that of the emperor. One of Gregory XV's last steps was the creation of the Congregation for the Propagation of the Faith, entrusted with the control of Catholic missions throughout the world.

The next pope, Urban VIII (1623–44) was of an entirely different stamp. He belonged to the great Florentine family of the Barberini. To his great culture was added the liveliest interest in politics and even in the military arts, for he was an expert on fortifications, of such importance at that period that knowledge of them formed part of the accomplishments of every man of gentle birth. In organizing the defence of the Papal States and in strengthening their military power, he showed clearly his conviction that this was the hour when it was imperative for the sword to be put to the service of the spirit. As a former nuncio in France he was inclined to favour that country rather than the Empire or Spain. However, from the beginning he had trouble with France over the Valteline affair and found himself in a delicate position with Richelieu who, underestimating the Protestant danger in Germany, was giving priority to the destruction of the House of Austria. Urban VIII, on the contrary, was so conscious of the danger that he refused to help in the application of the Edict of Restitution, made in the pontificate of Gregory XV by the Emperor Ferdinand II, which ordered that, throughout the Empire, all ecclesiastical possessions taken from the Catholics since 1555 must be restored to them. Urban was afraid that this would lead to a violent reaction from the whole of Protestant Germany. It can be seen that the political realism of Richelieu and the prudence of the pope were moving in the same direction and it is possible to understand the bitter feelings of the imperialists after the triumphs of Gustavus Adolphus. Although, in this singularly complicated situation, Urban VIII, anxious to act as the common father of all Christians, made great efforts to bring about peace between the two camps, his temporal authority was gravely affected and the harm done was permanent.

The hostility of the Jansenists, blunders such as the condemnation of Galileo, rivalry, leading to war, between the Farnese and the Barberini, also diminished the authority of the pope, great as he was for his apostolic zeal, and renowned also for the baroque splendours which he gave in profusion to the Eternal City, though in doing so, he sacrificed irreplaceable legacies of earlier ages.

To what extent the voice of the supreme head of the Church had been weakened in temporal matters can be seen under Innocent X (1644–55), at the conclusion of the Westphalian Treaties. The balance of power in Europe, achieved by these treaties, had indeed, as corollaries, the proclaimed equality of Catholic and Protestant worship and the supremacy of the civil power in religious matters. The pope's immediate protest (in his Bull, *Zelus domus meae*) was of no effect, as were, save in the realm of conscience, the condemnations which followed. For the magisterium of the Church, an epoch had come to an end.

By saying that, it is not intended to give the impression that the Church had previously been undisputed mistress in the religious field. Her struggles with the civil power took place in every age but the quarrel between priesthood and Empire is one of the most striking examples. The difference is, however, that between episodic crises and a permanent state of affairs. It is at this juncture that the relations between the Roman Church and the nations should be studied from the point of view of the movement of the latter towards religious autonomy, as in France with Gallicanism and later in Germany with Josephism. This outline of the question has been deliberately left to the end of this chapter so as not to break the thread of the general argument.

The wish for autonomy had been one of the aspects of the Reformation, and, at the moment when the latter had established its position in part of Europe, it could have been considered that national Churches were a lesser evil and that the essence was saved. But we must not judge this with our twentieth-century mentality, based on recent definitions by the Church, notably on conciliar matters; rather must we appreciate that it was possible then, without bad faith, to be unaware of the terrible danger to which unity of belief was exposed by allowing the clergy of a nation to set limits to the authority of Rome. In any case, Gallicanism, or similar movements in other countries, did not take these extreme views, and all that was done was to impose on the clergy a political conformity, of little danger to the faith, or, less dangerous still, it was Parliament which stirred up the quarrel to serve its own interests.

In the first half of the seventeenth century, this tendency was most marked in France. The wars of religion ought, in principle, to have rallied Catholics round the papacy, but public opinion blamed the latter for the mistake of supporting Spain. The outrages of the Leaguers, and of the regicides, who were thought to have been incited by the Spaniards, did the rest, even among the lower classes. In such a field, it is not surprising that the policy of Richelieu, in whom the statesman silenced the scruples of the cardinal, bore such doubtful fruit. But it must be recognized, in all fairness, that he was playing an extremely difficult part and admiration must perhaps be given to his skill in compromise, by which, at one and the same time, he resisted the political interference of Rome but kept under the authority of the pope a clergy given to yearnings for independence. A good example of his method is his attitude towards Edmond Richer and Fr Santarelli, S.J.

Edmond Richer (1559–1633), a syndic at the Sorbonne, had published in 1611 a short treatise called *De ecclesiastica et politica potestate*, in which he distinguished between the executive power given to the pope over the whole Church and to the bishops over their dioceses and the legislative power belonging to General Councils and to diocesan synods. This amounted to an assertion of the superiority of the Council over the pope and left the field clear for national Churches. Gallicanism, which would have put the theories of Richer into practice, was not to Richelieu's taste; it would have made the French episcopate into a kind of parliament difficult to handle. The cardinal, with the help of Fr Joseph, forced the author of the publication to retract. But Richelieu was no more anxious for the authority of the Holy See to increase in France. Fr Santarelli had published in Rome a work in total opposition to Gallican tendencies. Parliament not only seized the book but ordered all the Jesuits in Paris to disown it. Richelieu limited this obligation to the superiors of houses who had to sign or leave the country.

The solution, which Richelieu had in mind, was the one he inspired in Pierre de Marca, as given in the latter's book *De Concordia Sacerdotii et Imperii*, published in 1641. This work imposed limits on the infallibility of the pope and left a place for the divine right of kings in the ecclesiastical field. This book was condemned in Rome, as was that of Rabardeau, which called for a patriarchate in France, which was to be held by Richelieu. This extraordinary proposal was probably an attempt to manoeuvre Rome rather than a concrete intention. But those who launch an idea upon the world cannot hope to keep it in their control, and when in the course of the next half century the Church in France contrived to avoid lapsing into schism it was only by a narrow margin, as we shall see.

CHAPTER II

CHRISTIAN THOUGHT
AND THE
HUMANIST LEGACY

The Middle Ages studied ancient times with the light of the
faith as a guide. Then came the Renaissance, a debatable
term but one which may be retained here, as it expresses quite
well the blossoming forth of Greco-Roman thought in the
field of the sciences, arts and letters. The pagan gods were
revived, though in a symbolic setting, but they exercised a
certain seduction, as did, with their classical beauty, the whole
of ancient culture and philosophy, henceforward to be practised for their own sake. In the sixteenth century, under the
influence of the Reformation, many minds had already crossed
the neutral zone separating private judgement from free
thought. This explains at the beginning of the seventeenth
century, after the "Que sais-je?" of Montaigne, the success of
stoicism, which had its followers in Germany before passing
into France; traces of it can be perceived in Corneille, Christian though he was. Similarly, the progress of Epicureanism
can be explained; its adherents were many in England,
Italy and France, from the upright man, who wished to link
with antiquity a pleasant conception of life, down to the
Hedonists and Libertines—Lord Herbert of Cherbury, Vanini,
Campanella, Théophile de Viau and so on.

However, care must be taken not to attribute an exclusive influence to the continuance of humanism. The autonomy of Cartesianism, which was beginning at this period, was certainly effective in detaching theology from philosophy and the sciences. If Descartes did not submit matters of faith to systematic questioning, he had a strong misgiving that others would do so, while others again, in all sincerity, would not be able to put such restraint on themselves. On this point, at which the orthodoxy of Malebranche, the Oratorian, wavered, the way lay open also to Deism or unbelief, and the following century was definitely to follow it.

Finally, scientific progress often provoked a similar reaction, since new discoveries seemed to throw doubt on a truth revealed but not fully understood. The most famous example is the condemnation of Galileo, due to a too literal interpretation of Scripture. Nevertheless, the new attitude in scientific research was to be of great benefit to theological science at a much later date.

For the moment, however, the Church worked on its old resources, and this field, cultivated with fresh zeal, gave a splendid harvest to this half-century. In scholastic theology the work was due to a group of Discalced Carmelites of Alcala, the *Complutenses*, which was followed by that of the Carmelites of Salamanca, the *Salamanticenses*, the most complete work in existence of the Thomist school. French theologians, whose inclination was rather to patristics and textual criticism, also produced works of great value, such as the *Dogmata theologica* of Denis Petau of the Collège of Clermont, and the works of André Duval and Nicolas Cornet of the Sorbonne, and of that great "debunker" of saints, Abbé de Launoy, of the College of Navarre.

As a consequence of improved religious observance, of the problems of conscience raised by Protestantism and of the tendencies from which Jansenism was to emerge, many books of spiritual direction and of casuistry were published. The seventeenth century has been called the golden age of spiritual direction. That is true, especially of France, and it is not surprising that a generation which enjoyed *La Princesse de Clèves* should have attached sufficient importance to problems of conscience to seek advice and enlightenment. St Francis de Sales was the model of spiritual direction; his discreet authority sought to make the Christian capable of standing on his own feet. Almost all the instigators of clerical reform, mentioned in the following chapter, added spiritual direction to their other activities. In addition, mention should be made of Fr Louis Lallemant. In moral theology the name of Escobar, the Spanish Jesuit, must not be passed over, despite his somewhat unjust treatment by Pascal.

This same development in spirituality has left its mark in the field of ascetic and mystic theology. Here, mention must again be made of St Francis de Sales. Anxious to win over heretics, and also to draw towards God a society which was growing increasingly refined, he gave to the service of religion a style of charming gentleness and simplicity, making it attractive without detracting in any way from its august nature. His *Treatise on the Love of God*, his *Introduction to the Devout Life* and, addressed to the Reformers, his *Controversies*, form part of our literary treasure and served to popularize an already known religious ideal.

It is quite another thing with a generation of priests who, imbued with the grandeur of the priesthood, through which the mission of Christ is perpetuated, obtained from the teaching of St Paul and the Fathers of the Church a spirituality wonderfully adapted to their period. We shall see, later on, in connection with the Catholic Renaissance in France, their apostolic and charitable work. But, on the purely spiritual plane, the names of Cardinal de Bérulle, also a friend of St Francis de Sales, and his cult of the Word Incarnate, the reason for man's existence, of Père de Condren, with his emphasis on the resurrection of Christ, and of Jean-Jacques

Olier who felt deeply the mystery of the Eucharist and spread devotion to it, should all be mentioned. They made a mark on their times, not only among the clergy but also in a lay society much concerned with religious matters.

Christian erudition also became more exacting to keep pace with the development of the critical spirit. There was progress in exegesis; progress, owing to archeological excavations (in the catacombs), in knowledge of the primitive Church; progress in discovering and listing the episcopal and monastic past of France, owing to the *Gallia Christiana* of the two Fathers de Sainte-Martha, and afterwards of the Maurists. Finally, progress in hagiography, begun by Fr Rosweyde of Douai. From his work emerged that of the Bollandists with their *Acta Sanctorum* worthy, from the first volume published in 1643, to be taken as models of patient and scrupulous research.

CHAPTER III

CATHOLIC RENAISSANCE
IN FRANCE

In the previous century, it was from Spain and Italy, untouched by the Reformation, that the great Catholic revival had sprung, whereas then France was utterly divided, although it was destined later to play its part magnificently, and that for many reasons, among which should be mentioned, first of all, the pacificatory work of Henri IV. In any case it should not be underestimated, although it was possible and fruitful only because it corresponded with an intellectual evolution. Indeed, if the country accepted a compromise solution in its religious policies, this was not solely due to lassitude and a desire for peace. It was also because Catholicism was there so much of a living reality that the Protestants considered themselves fortunate in the situation in which they found themselves, on the one hand, and the Catholics, on the other, were no longer uneasy about the future. Forty years earlier, such a compromise would have split France in two. How had this change come about? To a small degree perhaps, as is sometimes said, because the Reformation appeared to many people like a leaven of political and intellectual anarchy. In this respect the national character should be taken into consideration, but to a large extent it was due to the fact that a new spirituality had penetrated the country from Spain and Italy. To understand to what degree the writings of St Teresa

and of St John of the Cross, the example of St Aloysius
Gonzaga, the work of St Charles Borromeo and of St Philip
Neri had been able to influence matters, it is enough to recall
the cultural links which, independently of political upheavals,
had been formed between the two Latin sisters. Indeed, it
would have been strange if this spiritual movement had
remained on the other side of the mountains, when the French
language, theatre and social customs were being increasingly
inspired by Spain and Italy, and when the kings of France
sought their queens or their ministers in those countries.

The great figures just mentioned belong to the previous
period. The link between the two centuries is to be found in
St Francis de Sales (1567–1622), who has already been quoted
as a religious writer; the whole range of his activity must now
be described. As bishop of Geneva he was able better than
anyone else to appreciate the needs of the times. During his
mission in Chablais, he showed how by peaceful methods, it
was possible to recall Protestants to the Roman faith;
and, in France, it was Catholics themselves whom he led
back to their religious practice by a method which was mild
and persuasive at the same time. It would be a mistake to
depict him as exclusively devoted to a mission to fashionable
society, since one of his main preoccupations, in which he
was able to fix the interest of Henri IV, was training of the
clergy. But it is certain that he was one of the forerunners of
what is now called Catholic Action. The Order of the Visitation, which he founded with the Baroness de Chantal (1572–
1641), had originally been, in its conception, a charitable
association, open even to married women, for devout retire-
ment, and included, along with manual works, visitation of the
sick, hence its name. It was in obedience to the archbishop of
Lyons, who was too timorous, that Francis de Sales agreed,
much against his wish, to make it into a real religious Order
which, moreover, achieved considerable expansion under his
direction. If seventeenth-century French society, particularly

in the reign of Louis XIII, was so clearly distinguished by a profound religious tendency among so many of the laity, this is due, in large measure, to St Francis de Sales. The Company of the Blessed Sacrament, founded long after his day, and even the Gentlemen of Port-Royal, sprang from the spirit he had been able to create. From him dates also the admission of women to the apostolate, one of the characteristic features of that age.

Very different, but as important in the same direction, was the work of the Jesuits as confessors and educators. Banished by the Parliament of Paris for political reasons, they were allowed to return by the Edict of Rouen (1603), and in their colleges, which rapidly prospered, they exercised almost a monopoly over the education of noble and middle-class youth. The influence exerted by Fr Coton, his confessor, on Henri IV is well known, as is also how many great minds came from the College of La Flèche, founded by the king.

However, all this progress would not have satisfied the Christian ideal had it been limited to the privileged classes. It still had to reach the mass of the people, and a huge task there awaited the clergy who were, unfortunately, far inferior to the work required of them. The clerical renewal achieved by missionaries and organizers of admirable worth is another essential characteristic of this half-century. What was, indeed, the state of the clergy prior to this? In spite of real efforts made since the Council of Trent, they needed drastic reform spiritually even more than in their corporate structure. This indeed was solid enough. As the first order in the kingdom, owning immense wealth, especially in landed property, the clergy was a political, financial and social power. Its Assembly, held every five years, voted a contribution to the king which, though voluntary in principle, was one of his surest sources of income. But, in the spiritual field, the ineffectiveness of so strongly organized a body is striking.

Consider, first, the condition of the secular clergy. The higher clergy, bishops and holders of large benefices, were nominated by the king. As they were mainly younger sons of noble families, often without a vocation, they led a worldly life, when they were not living at court. In the lower clergy, the miserable incumbents were obliged to hand over the best part of their income from the parish to the owners of the great tithes. Frequently, they were distracted from their ministry by anxiety to ensure their material subsistence. Many were ignorant and some lived disorderly lives. All these deficiencies were known in Rome, but Rome was powerless, as the king and parliament, very anxious to avoid papal encroachments, were opposed to the application in France of the canons of the Council of Trent.

Help came first from the bishops. If it can be said that some of its representatives were hardly qualified to insist on the practice of virtues of which they were incapable of giving an example themselves, it was, however, the bishops who first took action in the States General of 1614. This was to lead to the acceptance of the Council of Trent by the assembly of clergy in 1615. The rôle of the hierarchy, as has recently been shown by Fr Blet, was a decisive one.

Next, help came from priests who, convinced of the need for education of the clergy and bearing in mind the prescriptions of the Council of Trent, accomplished it by means of seminaries. The first of these priests was Pierre de Bérulle (1575-1629). On November 11th, 1611, in a house in the Faubourg Saint-Jacques, he gathered together six priests, who, without taking monastic vows, decided to devote themselves entirely to the attainment of the priestly ideal, by uniting their lives with that of Christ himself, the great high priest. Bérulle had not envisaged, at the beginning, setting up seminaries, but his was the first step in that direction, and subsequently it became the main task of the Oratory, the Congregation which he had established. Furthermore, invited by Rome to extend their activities, the Oratorians helped the parish priests in every way. Some specialized in erudition, others in preaching, and their colleges were the most important, after those of the Jesuits.

The work of Bérulle was continued by his worthy successor, Charles de Condren (1588–1641), and by two disciples whom it is only necessary to name to evoke the diversity of their work: Adrien Bourdoise (1584–1665), an innovator from rural surroundings, supporter of a communal life for the secular clergy and restorer of the parochial spirit, who founded a seminary in his parish, St Nicolas du Chardonnet; and then St Jean Eudes (1601–80), founder of the Congregation of Jesus and Mary, and of seminaries in Normandy.

Although he never belonged to the Oratory but was a friend of Bérulle, St Vincent de Paul represents the same ideal, helped by good common sense and a spirit of initiative, which made him one of the great organizers of religious and social life of the seventeenth century. Of humble origins, but becoming a priest after good solid studies, he had, as parish priest first of Clichy and then of a small parish in Bresse, already given proof of his value among the poor when he was called to be chaplain to Queen Marguerite de Valois, and later tutor to the Gondi family. These connections, added to his own ability, enabled him to found, in 1618, the confraternity of the Ladies of Charity, and, in 1625, a society of missionaries for country people. In 1632, the latter took the name of the Congregation of Priests of the Mission, with their mother house at the priory of Saint-Lazare from whence the name of Lazarists given to the religious of this congregation (in English-speaking countries they are known as Vincentians). Anxious at the same time about the training of the secular clergy, he instituted, at Saint-Lazare, retreats in preparation for ordination; the Tuesday conferences, for priests already at work in the ministry, and, finally, in 1642, the seminary of the Bons-Enfants.

It was, in fact, a member of the Tuesday conferences, a man about town called to the priesthood, Jean-Jacques Olier, more usually known as Monsieur Olier, who founded at Vaugirard, in 1642, a seminary reserved to those who had received a classical education; this was later moved to Saint-Sulpice, of which Olier was appointed parish priest. He inspired in them a desire for a high degree of perfection. This was the origin of the Society of Priests of Saint-Sulpice, whose activity was wholly devoted to the training of priests, and whose seminaries rapidly increased in the provinces and in Canada. Monsieur Olier also exerted great influence by his model organization of his parish and by the effective catechistic work which he entrusted to his seminarists.

This apostolic action had its counterpart in the provinces in the form of veritable missions, where the untiring preachers were Le Nobletz and Blessed Julien Maunoir in Brittany, St Jean Eudes in Normandy, St Pierre Fourier in Lorraine, St Francis Regis in the Vivarais and the Cévennes, where the Protestant communities were very numerous. It is not possible to enumerate all the developments but they represent a unique combination in the religious history of France. A renewal among the regular clergy accompanied this revival and, here again, it must be admitted that this was painfully essential.

At a time when life was usually very hard, many monasteries had become havens of an easy life, if not worse. This evil was notorious, as the literature of the period clearly shows. The sincere piety of Louis XIII was upset by these disorders and, with his help, Cardinal François de la Rochefoucauld, a very great prelate over whom St Charles Borromeo had certainly exerted great influence, set about the work of reform. Already, immediately after the States General of 1614, this La Rochefoucauld had shown how courageous he was by persuading the assembly of the clergy to observe the canons of the Council of Trent, in spite of the Gallican tendencies of the government and Parliament. At Clairvaux and at Cîteaux, the malpractices and the resistance to change were such that reform was imperfectly achieved and, henceforward, a distinction had to be made between the religious of strict observance and those of common observance. For the former, mention must be made of the part played by Dom Denis Largentier, abbot of Cîteaux, and by Jean de la Barrière, commendatory abbot of the Feuillants. At Cluny, and with the Premonstratensians, energetic abbots were more successful. But the greatest success of Cardinal de la Rochefoucauld was the reform of the Canons Regular. He had been named by the king, abbot of Sainte-Geneviève and, with the help of twelve religious, chosen for their zeal, he made this house the centre of a Congregation of France, which numbered nearly one hundred monasteries. The work of the Canons of Sainte-Geneviève continued into the next century and two souvenirs of it still remain in Paris: the library of Sainte-Geneviève and the church of the same name, which was disaffected and is now the Panthéon.

In the Orders of Women, this was the period of important foundations, but still more so of the introduction into France of Congregations founded in other countries in the sixteenth-century. For instance, the Carmelites and the Ursulines, the establishment of which in France was due to Madame Acarie. The influence in French society of the women's teaching Orders must not be underestimated, such as the Canonesses of Notre-Dame and the Daughters of Notre-Dame, whose foundress St Jeanne de Lestonnac was Montaigne's niece.

Possibly in no other epoch in France was it more clearly understood that faith is of no avail without charity. There is no doubt that this virtue found abundant opportunities for its practice, and that the great poverty and wretchedness were heartrending in a half-century in which religious wars, the Thirty Years War, and the Fronde caused multiple ruins and epidemics.

St Vincent de Paul again appears at this time, as his work of charity was the most widespread and the most remarkable, revealing a genius for organization, a sense of social action and an ingenuity, all quite remarkable. From 1618, when still parish priest of Châtillon-les-Dombes, he created the first of his charity confraternities, in which noble ladies, married and unmarried, devoted themselves, each on their day, to corporal and spiritual care of the sick. Great-hearted women vied in good works, and, in Paris itself, the highest names soon figured among those who called themselves "the servants of the poor". Their work was devoted to the unfortunate of every kind, in hospitals, in prisons, and in the adoption of abandoned infants. The many-sided activities of "Monsieur Vincent" make one think of the most modern big-business men. When Théophraste Renaudot is discussed as the founder of the French Press, it is forgotten that the *Magasin charitable*, published by St Vincent to report cases of distress and to announce the help to be given, was a contemporary of the *Gazette*. Free soup kitchens, buying of herds, distribution of seeds, building of workshops, and of shelters, all these methods of social assistance were tried by him, and his solicitude for galley slaves and prisoners is well known.

The name of Louise de Marillac remains connected with that of St Vincent de Paul. It is to their joint initiative that is due the foundation in 1633 of the Sisters of Charity; they were originally recruited from humble country families to ensure more continuity of the services to which the Ladies of Charity could devote themselves only intermittently. It was only in 1642 that he allowed them to take annual vows, on condition that they remained in the world. The Sisters of Charity were only approved by Rome in 1668, when Monsieur Vincent had then been dead for eight years. It would be wrong to imagine that the virtues of this great saint made light of obstacles, for his life was ever one of struggle. For instance, during the Fronde, he had the audacity to ask the Queen

Mother to send Mazarin away, the only way, in his opinion, to restore peace, and the people were angry with him for having failed.

It is this same spirit, which would nowadays be called Catholic Action, which inspired the Duke of Ventadour, in 1627, with the idea of forming an association of piety, apostolate and charity, which later became the Company of the Blessed Sacrament. The nature of this organization, little known until recent times, aroused certain suspicions. However, it had the benefit of the advice of the most orthodox ecclesiastics of that time, such as Fr de Condren and Fr Suffren. Its secrecy is explained by a wish for efficiency, and, it must also be said, by a distrust of the authorities, who might have been tempted to make use of so powerful a league. It was also this wish to be independent that induced it to exclude from among its members all regular priests while other ecclesiastics, and not the least important, were members in great numbers. It may well be thought that it played an important part from the Catholic and social points of view. Its religious activity is shown by the development of the worship of the Blessed Sacrament, by its contribution towards the seemly upkeep of churches and the good behaviour of the clergy, and by the struggle against Protestantism and Jansenism. Its social work was marked by its help to hospitals, its aid to prisoners, the protection of girls, the suppression of evil haunts, and, among the nobility, suppression of the duel. Its initiative on this last point certainly earned for the Company very great hostility. It had against it the Jansenists, parliament and the authorities, who were disturbed by an activity over which they had no control. Meetings of the Company were forbidden in 1660 and nothing is known of its activities after 1666. But there is little doubt that its spirit lived on after the organization was proscribed, and that the remainder of the century was influenced by it, up to, and including the *Cabale des Dévots*.

Among the chief moving spirits of the Company of the Blessed Sacrament must be mentioned Baron de Renty who, with the shoemaker Henry Buch, worked to develop the professional religious confraternities. Both of them worked very efficiently to raise the morale of the workers, and to put an end to the secret actions of the *Compagnons du Devoir*, whose foul practices and revolutionary spirit were doing much harm.

CHAPTER IV

THE CATHOLIC RENAISSANCE IN ITALY AND SPAIN

Italy had not been shaken, like France, by the Wars of Religion, and the seventeenth century was relatively a tranquil period for her. The movement of religious renewal had begun there immediately after the Council of Trent, and it followed the work so splendidly begun by St Charles Borromeo and St Philip Neri, without exhibiting, therefore, a spectacle of heroic changes, such as had been carried through on the other side of the Alps. As if the absence of obstacles were making virtue a little sluggish, mystical developments themselves were rarer there. On the other hand, the Christian City was calmly perfecting its organization, through practical works, like those of the Regular Clerks, ministers of the sick, founded by St Camillus de Lellis, or those of the Celestial Annunciades, who helped the clergy by their works; or, again, by monumental works of erudition such as the *Annales ecclesiastici* of Baronius and of his successors.

It was not that the Catholic faith was sheltered from all attack. In Venice, for instance, the resistance of the Council of Ten to pontifical authority was supported by the Servite, Paolo Sarpi, author of a distorted history of the Council of Trent. He, backed by the English ambassador, had secret leanings towards Calvinism. The intervention of France and also of Spain brought about a reconciliation between the Republic and the Holy See, and all Protestant danger was removed from Italy (1607).

In Spain, as in Italy, the Church was living, so to speak, on the impulse given to it by the sixteenth century, and it was still reaping the benefit of the influence of St Ignatius Loyola and of St Teresa. The *Treatise on Christian Perfection,* by the Jesuit, Alphonsus Rodriguez, inspired even the recluses of Port Royal. Another Jesuit, St Peter Claver (†1654), became the apostle and defender of the Negroes of the New World. As for the Carmelites, whose work has been mentioned earlier, they founded a number of houses, in this half-century, both for men and for women, inside and outside the Peninsula.

A little more than a century had then elapsed since Spain had triumphed over the Moslems living in the south of its territory. The expulsion of the Moors in 1609 (that is, of the people of Moslem stock, who were still numerous and unassimilated), completed religious unity. It did not, however, prevent the nearness of the infidels from being always a grave anxiety to Spain. The ransoming of captives was the main purpose of the Order of the Trinity, which, under Bd John Baptist of the Conception, gave birth to a separate community, that of the Discalced Trinitarians, soon to be spread throughout Europe. Bd Mary Anne of Jesus founded about the same time the Discalced Nuns of Our Lady of Ransom who, in their prayers, associated themselves with the activities of the Trinitarians.

In the Low Countries, Spain had just lost its Northern Provinces, which had become completely Calvinistic, but in the Southern Provinces, notably due to the action of the Archdukes Albert and Isabella, Catholicism was very much alive. This region even became one of the main bulwarks of the Roman Faith, from which missionary activity reached out over England and the United Provinces.

CHAPTER V

PROTESTANTS AND CATHOLICS IN CENTRAL AND NORTHERN EUROPE

At the beginning of the seventeenth century, religious peace between Catholics and Protestants in Germany was based, in principle, on the "religious peace of Augsburg", which had begun a régime of compromise, to the details of which it is not proposed to return here. This solution was all the more unsatisfactory because both parties looked on it as no more than a waiting period and it was in no way inspired by a spirit of tolerance but rather by the formula, *cujus regio ejus religio*, or in other words, "In a prince's country, the prince's religion". Under the weak Emperor Rudolph II (1576–1612), this division could not be strictly maintained even in the Hapsburg States, since, following a dispute with his brother, the Archduke Matthias, this Emperor was compelled to cede to the latter sovereignty over Austria, Hungary and Moravia (1608). In the course of this struggle, both of them, but especially Matthias, had made large concessions to the Protestant elements. In Bohemia, Rudolph, by royal letters patent of July 9th, 1609, granted to the Lutherans the freedom of conscience which was already enjoyed by the Moravians. Matters were almost the same in Silesia.

This situation did not prevent a Catholic revival taking place also in Germany. This was not a "counter-Reformation", in the sense of the term as it has been long in use. Actually it was not essentially an offensive against Protestantism but, rather, the normal consequence of a Catholic reformation, whose beginning can be attributed to the Council of Trent and the progress of Roman efforts; to the activities of the Jesuits and to the spirit of faith and apostolate which was developed by the most famous among them, St Peter Canisius (1521–97). He has been called the "Second Apostle of Germany" (St Boniface being the first).

As in France, Spain and Italy, new religious Orders began to flourish but the old Orders were reformed at that same time. The final achievement of this work is what is known as the observance of Melk, a federation of part of the monasteries of Germany, approved in 1625 by Urban VIII. Unfortunately, the Thirty Years War undermined this structure, although there remained some tendencies towards federation. There was also reorganization among the secular clergy, in which the training of future priests owed much to Bd Bartholomew Holzhauser (1613–58) of Salzburg, founder of the Bartholomites.

The rulers took a definite part in this revival but their anxiety to see unity of faith in their country often showed itself in ruthless measures. Such was the case with the archduke, a former pupil of the Jesuits of Ingolstadt, who was later to become the Emperor Ferdinand II.

In Switzerland, where successful results had been achieved in the previous century by St Charles Borromeo, religious feelings were running high, as is evidenced by the murder of St Fidelis of Sigmaringen, in 1622, by Calvinist peasants.

At this epoch, Germany was already enflamed, for growing antagonisms had resulted in tragedy. In the spring of 1606, after a Catholic procession at Donauwörth was interfered with by Protestants, the disturbance was punished by the town

being outlawed from the Empire and incorporated into
Bavaria. This severe repression, ordered by the emperor, supported by princes of note, seemed serious enough to his
Protestant vassals for them to decide to secede at the Diet
of Ratisbon in April, 1608. In the following month, under
the Elector Palatine, Frederick IV (1583–1610), there was
formed a Union of German Protestant Rulers from the South
and West, the Protestant Union, soon to be assured of the
support of France and of the United Provinces.

A year later, this group was opposed by a Catholic League,
of which the leading spirit was Duke Maximilian of Bavaria.
The conflict almost broke out in that same year on the subject of the Julich succession, but the war, to be known later
as the Thirty Years War, only began in 1618, in Bohemia.
Emperor Matthias (1612–19) sought to restrict the freedoms
which his brother Rudolph had granted to the Protestants,
and, as a consequence, an uprising took place in Prague (The
Defenestration of Prague). Matthias died in March, 1619. The
insurgents refused to recognize the new emperor and elected
the Calvinist Elector Palatine as king, Frederick V (1610–32).
The latter was subsequently elected emperor by a part of
Protestant Germany but he was beaten at the battle of the
White Hill, near Prague, on September 8th, 1620. Catholicism
was re-established in Bohemia, in Hungary and in the Pala-
tinate, and, following negotiations in which Gregory XV
played an essential part, the emperor transferred the Pala-
tinate to Maximilian of Bavaria. This transfer was important,
since it gave a majority to the Catholics in the electoral Diet,
in which, up to that moment, Catholics and Protestants had
been equal. In order to save the Protestant cause, the king of
Denmark intervened but he was unsuccessful (Treaty of
Lübeck, 1629). Emboldened by his victory, Ferdinand II
published an Edict of Restitution under which Protestants
were to make restitution to the Church of all secularized land,
and he also proposed to change the imperial constitution. The

Protestants were helped by the very ambitions of Ferdinand, as they caused anxiety to Catholic France and to Lutheran Sweden alike. From this came the entrance on the scene of Gustavus Adolphus and of Richelieu. The latter, we may be sure, was not acting as a defender of the Reformation but, for national reasons, he wished to prevent a Hapsburg hegemony by giving support to those German princes, whether Catholic or Protestant, who wished to resist it. The war finished by taking on the character of a struggle between France and Austria, ending in a French victory and the treaties of Westphalia (1648).

It is certainly the case that the policy of the popes, during this long conflict, was to exploit every opportunity given to the Church by the temporary successes of the Hapsburgs. They also did everything in their power to prevent Richelieu from joining forces with the Protestant rulers. It is also no less certain that they were able to resist numerous attempts by the emperors to dictate the policy of the Holy See. It was to the interest of the Church that there should be an end to the long-lasting antagonism between the two great Catholic dynasties and it was for the purpose of creating a community of interests between them that Urban VIII at one time envisaged a joint action by them against the Turks.

It was from Rome, also, that there came the first steps towards negotiations which resulted in the treaties of Westphalia. As a matter of fact, peace did not further the interests of Catholicism since, far from setting up a system of tolerance, it sanctioned the principle of State Churches and confirmed, and increased, the Protestant acquisition of secularized possessions. Consequently, the representative of the Holy See absented himself from the closing session and Innocent X protested against it in his Bull, *Zelo domus Dei*.

In Poland, where Protestantism had penetrated extensively, at any rate among the nobility (Calvinism in Little-Poland

and Lutheranism in Greater-Poland and in Lithuania, and also many other sects), the Catholic cause was helped by divisions amongst the Protestants. The Jesuits helped considerably in the recapture of lost ground, which earned them vigorous hostility, and the country again had a Catholic majority. This renaissance is shown by the large number of religious buildings which date from this period. On the other hand, the Duchy of Prussia, vassal to the king of Poland, had become an island of Protestantism, following the apostasy of Albert of Brandenburg.

In Sweden, a Catholic restoration seemed, at one moment, quite possible. This was when the king of Poland, Sigismund II, in 1592, succeeded to the throne of Sweden. But he was betrayed by his uncle, Charles of Sodermanland, who was his representative on the other side of the Baltic. On his side the latter had the advantage of national feeling mingled with Lutheranism against a sovereign of foreign origin. Charles became king in 1604 and his son was Gustavus Adolphus, in whom the Protestants found one of their most redoubtable champions. At this same period Denmark was experiencing, under Christian IV (1588–1648), a merciless persecution of Catholics. Priests caught in that country were punished with death and conversions were penalized with banishment and confiscation of possessions.

In England, the beginning of the seventeenth century was marked by missionary activity on the part of the Catholics, coming from the seminaries and colleges set up on the Continent during the second half of the previous century. Under Elizabeth, this had been met by savage legislation, which had resulted in many martyrdoms among priests and had forced Catholics to live in secrecy owing to confiscations, penalties or imprisonment.

On the death of Elizabeth, there was a moment of hope, as James VI of Scotland, who succeeded her under the title of James I of England, was the son of Mary Stuart, a Catholic.

Disillusionment was quick to follow. The Gunpowder Plot (1605), which may have been a Protestant ruse, succeeded in setting public feeling against the Catholics and enabled new measures to be taken against them. Among these appear the prohibition to follow certain professions and, above all, an oath of which the main condition was the denial of the right of the pope to depose a king. Paul V forbade this oath to be taken, which caused a division among the Catholics, especially as the king was engaged in controversy with Rome. Once the period of uncertainty had passed, the period of persecution continued, but executions became less numerous as the king, who was not as harsh as the Tudors, was relying on moderation to win over the Catholics and his financial needs made fines more acceptable. It can be said that, at that period, it was among the members of the House of Commons, particularly, that Catholics had their most dangerous enemies.

There was fresh hope on the accession of Charles I, who had married Henrietta of France. It had been agreed, at the marriage, that Catholics in England would be able to follow their religion, on condition that this was not done in public. It is hard to doubt the good faith of the king in this matter but he had to reckon with parliament and with public opinion largely hostile to this idea. Consequently, the Catholics were always being troubled, and even the queen herself found that her liberty to practise her religion was being contested, contrary to the marriage contract. To the conflict between king and parliament, which quickly became acute, there was added a religious conflict, since Puritans and other Protestant sects detested Anglicanism, the religion of which the king was head and which, in their eyes, retained too many elements of popery. There is no doubt that, faced with Puritan intransigence, Anglican compromise may have given Catholics some reason to hope, and, when the trial of strength began, on the revolt of the Scottish Presbyterians against the king, the majority of Catholics remained loyal to Charles. Whether it be that he looked on them as a trump card, or whether he had genuine sympathy with the Catholics, the king alleviated their lot so that, even in his own suite, there were conversions to Catholicism. He even went so far as to renew dealings with Rome where for some time it was hoped there might be an end to the schism. Obviously this attitude added one more argument for the opposition. The Civil War swept away the king and the Anglican church and, under the Puritan Commonwealth of Cromwell, Catholics had no choice but to go underground.

In Scotland, the situation of Catholics was at least as bad. Early on Protestantism had there taken the form of intransigent Presbyterianism and the anti-papist laws were more severe there than in England. There were not so many executions, but heavy fines and a much more generally hostile feeling. There did remain, however, some small islands of Catholicism, implying a remarkably strong faith; it may also be explained by the influence of great families, owners of vast domains. As in the case of England, seminaries and colleges on the Continent formed missionary centres, but they were few in number and provided only a small number of missionaries.

Ireland, on the whole, had remained faithful to Catholicism. The Dublin Parliament had, indeed, recognized the supremacy of the sovereign in religious affairs and the official religion was Anglicanism. But the parliament was mainly composed of English immigrants. The clergy and the people as a consequence were the more strongly attached to a faith which had become identified with national feelings. Executions and fines had little effect and an insurrection broke out. It was brutally suppressed and the English remained masters of the island in 1602. They introduced a régime of oppression, which showed itself in mass confiscations and in the settlement of English and Scottish Protestants in Ulster. Under obligation to support at their own expense their Catholic priests, the Irish had still to pay their tithes and rent to the Anglican clergy. There were, indeed, times when ecclesiastics had to flee the country under pain of death.

After a calmer period at the beginning of the reign of Charles I, Ireland again endured persecution under Strafford. When the conflict between king and parliament became acute, the Irish imagined that, in exchange for their loyalty, the king would grant them freedom to practise their faith. They were disappointed. In 1641, a terrible revolt occurred during which many English and many Scots from Ulster were massacred. During the Civil War and the Commonwealth, the English regained the upper hand at the price of frightful butchery, notably in 1649. The slaughter at Drogheda, a small town whose capture was followed by a hideous massacre, and at Wexford, are a blot on the memory of Cromwell. But then, what humane feelings could be expected from troops capable of inscribing on their standard the monstrous device of "Jesus and no quarter". An Act of Parliament, passed in 1652, confiscated the possessions of all the Irish Catholics, which were given to Protestants, with the Irish becoming tenants of the new owners. All the reward given to those who had not taken part in the rebellion was to grant them fresh land in the poorest province in the island, that of Connaught. The priests were forced to leave the country under pain of death. Thus continued the martyrdom of an island which, in the very early Middle Ages, had sent so many missionaries to the Continent. Thus between the English and the Irish a great barrier was erected.

It can well be imagined that the Holy See did not remain inactive during this tragedy. Action was taken at foreign courts, priests were sent, Jesuits particularly, and agents charged with the duty of maintaining the faith and keeping up courage, all of which helped in preserving what was best in Catholicism. As with England and Scotland, Irish colleges were founded on the Continent, whence came priests who in secret fought effectively against Anglican propaganda.

CHAPTER VI

MISSIONARY WORK IN THE NEAR EAST AND IN THE PAGAN WORLD

If the Reformation, a comparatively recent event, formed a major anxiety for the Church in the seventeenth century, it must not be imagined that the brethren, separated at a much earlier date, namely the Greeks, were neglected. From the time when the Turks had occupied the greater part of their country, the Greeks had been in a very precarious position. The rule of the sultan has sometimes been described as a very tolerant one, because it recognized the legality of the Greek Church and because the patriarch had even some temporal authority. In fact, Turkish officials contrived to paralyse the activities of the Greek clergy, and, in those places in which this clergy was especially ignorant or corrupt, they won the people over to Islam. It must be admitted, however, that on the whole the Greek Church was able to hold out and, as often happens, the Greeks owed it to their faith that they were able to maintain their identity. Probably the relative tolera-tion granted by the Turks, which would certainly not have continued in the event of a return to unity with Rome, may partly explain the failure of the steps taken by Rome for that purpose. But, primarily, the Greek Church was jealous of its independence, and it is only in the field of erudition, particularly in the works of Allarci, that these attempts have left any trace.

The Protestants also made efforts to win over the Greek Church but these were in vain. The only point of danger was with Patriarch Cyril Lukaris (1620–38), an ambitious Cretan very hostile to Rome, who had studied in Italy and then lived in Poland and in Lithuania. In 1629, he published a Calvinist confession of faith, which was very badly received, and he died tragically by strangling at the hands of the Turks.

Attempts were also made for union with the Russian Church. The most favourable opportunity seemed to have been offered by the appearance in Poland, in the year 1605, of one, Dimitry, who passed himself off as a son of Ivan IV. This person, whose real identity is still uncertain and who became a secret convert to Catholicism, managed to get himself crowned in Moscow, during the "time of troubles".

The Holy See, which was very much involved in this, felt that it was on the eve of a reunion of the Russian Church with Rome. Dimitry, by the pledges he soon gave to the schismatics, showed how false were the hopes that had been placed in him. He died soon afterwards, a victim of the hatred which his policy had aroused; and the Romanov dynasty, coming to power in 1613, adopted an attitude which discouraged any further attempt at union. The position of the Orthodox Church with regard to Rome and to the Protestants, was defined in 1638, by the Confession of Peter Mogila, Metropolitan of Kiev. The authority accorded to this text throughout the Greek Orient underlined the incompatibility of the various points of view.

The efforts made in the pagan world obtained results which were far more encouraging. It would, indeed, have been unpardonable if the Church, at a period of great internal restoration, had not shown anxiety to apply equal zeal to the propagation of the faith. Even considered from the numerical angle alone, it is a fact that the zeal of its missionaries more than compensated for the losses caused by the Reformation.

The necessary coordination was provided by Pope Gregory XV, who, in 1622, created the Congregation De Propaganda Fide, consisting of twenty-nine cardinals (this must not be confused with the Association for the Propagation of the Faith, founded in France exactly two centuries later, which has for its object the support of missions by the giving of alms). Its field for action was in pagan countries, and, at the same time, in those countries in which Protestantism was in power. In 1627, Urban VIII added to it a seminary in Rome, where missionaries of all nations were trained. A similar step led in 1663 to the foundation in Paris of the seminary for foreign missions (known as the Missions Étrangères).

It was in Asia and in the New World that the most remarkable work was done and the greatest results achieved.

In India, in the footsteps of St Francis Xavier, the Jesuits evangelized vast regions. At the beginning of the seventeenth century they had two provincialates there, but, fifty years later, there were four hundred Jesuits engaged in their evangelical work. Their success was due, in part, to the methods of Fr Robert de Nobili, who, after 1606, had taken the initiative of approaching the Hindu priests themselves, by adopting their way of life and being guided by some of their rules. This method, called Accommodation, had its critics but it received the express approval of Gregory XV in 1623. Later on, Nobili extended his missionary work to pariahs, an unfortunate caste which had hitherto been neglected. At his death, in 1656, the Christian mission in Madura was at the height of its prosperity, and, at the end of the century, the Christians there numbered 150,000.

Three obstacles then arose seriously to compromise this exceptionally successful undertaking. Other religious Orders, severely criticizing the accommodation method, demanded an inquiry and the prohibition of these successful practices. The decline of the Portuguese Empire and the over-ruling power of the English and Dutch nations in this part of the world restricted the liberty of Catholic undertakings. The final blow came, in 1773, with the suppression of the Jesuits.

Before the seventeenth century only isolated attempts had been made in Indo-China. There also, the Jesuits worked with great success and history remembers the names of Fr Buzoni in Cochin-China and of Fr Alexander of Rhodes in Annam. The latter played some part in the steps which led to the creation of the Paris seminary for Foreign Missions and he it was who, taking his inspiration from the Latin alphabet, gave to the Annamites the letters which they still use today. In 1660, it was reckoned that there were about 350,000 Christians in Indo-China but terrible persecutions soon made havoc of this work.

The methods of Peter de Nobili had already been practised in China by another Jesuit, Fr Matteo Ricci (1532–1610), by Fr Schall († 1666) and by the Flemish Fr Verbiest († 1688). By adopting Chinese dress, by even allowing the ancestor cult, by cultivating the language of the country and by putting their scientific knowledge at the service of the nobles and even of the court, they acquired great prestige and obtained a large number of conversions. Unfortunately, as in India, these methods were vigorously attacked by other religious, Franciscans and Dominicans; this antagonism had deplorable results, especially when Rome forbade a large number of Chinese practices. Equally disastrous was the fall of the Ming dynasty in 1644. Its rulers had maintained excellent relations with the Jesuits, and the last of their line, who held out for only a short time in South China, was baptized along with his family. The Manchu invasion was the signal for massacres and persecution, which considerably reduced the number of Christians. It has been estimated, possibly with some exaggeration, that there were, at one time, nearly a million of them, with a certain number of native priests. At the beginning of the nineteenth century, there were only 200,000 of them at the very most. In any case, it must not be thought that the progress of Christianity had always been peaceful before the Manchu conquest, as many missionaries were martyred even in that period.

In Japan, missionary history in the seventeenth century is a quick-moving drama. It was an alternation of ferocious persecutions and magnificent triumphs, but also of dreadful blunders, among which deserving special condemnation is the jealousy, mentioned above, of the Jesuits shown by other religious Orders. The most harmful were the Spanish Franciscans, coming from the Philippine Islands. At the end of the previous century, twenty-six Christians, including some children, had been crucified in Nagasaki. Later on, a remarkable increase had raised the number of Christians in Japan to half a million, but, after 1614, the greed of English and Dutch business men induced them to intimate to the Shogun that the Portuguese and Spanish missionaries were only the forerunners of a conquest of Japan. The result of this treachery was that the missionaries were driven out, the churches were destroyed and persecutions followed, each more violent than the last. The most terrible persecution took place in 1624, when there were 30,000 victims in one year. In 1640, entry into Japan was forbidden to Christians and this remained the rule for more than two centuries afterwards. Alone, Dutch traders of the Protestant faith were allowed to enter, and a certain symbolic value can be attached to the obligation laid down on them, according to tradition, of walking on a crucifix before being authorized to disembark.

Reference has been made above to the Philippines, where, out of two million inhabitants, probably one half of them were Catholics. But these were poor Catholics, with little instruction in their faith.

The work of the Church in America shows quite a different character. In those countries dependent on Spain, missionaries were directly helped by the Crown and of course had not to placate more or less hostile authorities. In Peru, the early years of the seventeenth century were also the last years in the life of St Turibius (1538–1606), who has been compared with St Charles Borromeo; he founded many hospitals, seminaries and missions. This is also the country of St Francis Solano and of St Rose of Lima.

Peru was especially the field of action of the Franciscans and Dominicans, and, to a lesser degree, of the Jesuits. On the other hand, it was the Jesuits who did the greater part of the work for religion in Brazil and Paraguay. It is not enough to say religious work only, as their activity spread over all fields, and they may well be claimed as the creators of the Brazilian nation.

But it was in Paraguay that the sons of St Ignatius exerted a still more powerful and more original influence. It originated in their wish to protect the Indian population from the exploitation and moral corruption to which the settlers subjected them. After 1609, with the support of the Spanish Government, the Jesuits gathered the Indians together in Christian villages, called "Reductions". In principle, the natives administered their affairs themselves, but in reality they were under the friendly care of the Fathers, who organized a veritable Christian republic in Paraguay, based on collective property and a common agricultural policy. It was a patriarchal régime, the inspiration for which can be found in Sir Thomas More's *Utopia*, and in a work published at exactly the same time as these "Reductions" were begun, namely, the *Civitas Solis* of the Dominican, Thomas Companella, a real forerunner of collectivism.

In South America, in the first half of the seventeenth century, there were five archbishoprics, twenty-seven bishoprics and hundreds of monasteries, covering all the regions to which

European civilization had penetrated. But there were shadows in the picture, too; for example, the fate of the negroes who were imported to do the heavy work for which the Indians had proved unsuitable. Their wretched state aroused the charitable zeal of the Jesuit, St Peter Claver (1580–1654), who worked in Cartagena for almost half a century. Another black spot was the slight interest, not to put too hard a word on it, that was taken in the recruitment of a native clergy.

In Central America, in Mexico, in the West Indies, there was the same missionary success. Coming from Mexico, the Jesuits established themselves in California and there exerted an influence comparable to that which they obtained in Paraguay. They were followed by the Franciscans.

In North America, which escaped Spanish domination, a very large variety of organizations shared in the missionary work—Jesuits, Franciscans, Dominicans, Sulpicians and priests of the Paris Foreign Missions. But difficulties were incomparably greater there than in Latin America. The natives were much less manageable and there was Protestant hostility to be contended with. The Jesuits, it seems, did the most effective work both in Canada and also to the west of the English Colonies; in Wisconsin and Illinois. The best-known of their martyrs were Fr Jean de Brébeuf, Fr Isaac Jogues and their companions, who were massacred by the Hurons and the Iroquois between 1646 and 1649. At the same period, a gentleman from La Flèche, Jerome de la Dauversière, inspired by Monsieur Olier, founded Montreal, with the help of the Sulpicians, thus beginning the peopling of Canada and of Acadia by the French, mainly from their Western regions. The Recollect Franciscans who had been driven out of these districts by the English in 1629, were to return there towards 1670.

Africa was clearly the most neglected continent and so it remained until the nineteenth century. It was not that zeal was lacking, as was proved by the hundreds of Franciscans and Dominicans who were martyred in North Africa, but

Islam was particularly hostile there to Christianity. In addition to the Mercedarians who, it will be remembered, ransomed Cervantes from captivity, the Vincentians succeeded in setting up actual parishes in the prisons and hulks, where Christians were working, and they even succeeded in getting the Berber authorities to admit chaplains to work with the European consuls. Proof of the great opposition shown by Islam is to be found in the failure of the apostolate in Mozambique where Mohammedans were numerous, whereas in the Congo, the Capuchins had some success and obtained the nomination of a prefect apostolic.

In Abyssinia, where the religion was a monophysite Christianity, there was great hope when the priests abjured their heresy, but only to revert to it very quickly and finally. In Madagascar, the Vincentians failed but their effort was not completely fruitless: the seed, having been sown, germinated at a later date.

PART II

THE CHURCH, ABSOLUTE GOVERNMENTS AND THE GREAT DOCTRINAL DISPUTES IN THE SECOND HALF OF THE SEVENTEENTH CENTURY

The seventeenth century, in its first half, was characterized by the trial of strength between the Catholic world and the Reformation. This contest had ended in a state of balance, which absolutism had finally made applicable both politically and doctrinally. It had become very difficult for the Church to regain its lost ground, but its losses had been in some measure recompensed by a remarkable Catholic revival. In the second half of the century, the absolutism reached its highest point of achievement. In France, particularly, politics encroached on religion to such an extent that the popes themselves had to make terms with the king. At one time it was feared that national Churches would be established, thus coming to the very brink of schism. At that same period, although the situation regarding the Reformation could be considered as stabilized, dangerous doctrines and disturbing philosophies, such as Jansenism and Quietism, could be seen developing in the heart of the Church; they gravely compromised not only unity of faith but faith itself. These divisions, indeed, led to the growth of scepticism, and already there were clear signs of the strong current of rationalism, which was to be one of the great features of the eighteenth century.

CHAPTER VII

THE CHURCH AND THE
TEMPORAL POWER

If the Church had based its hopes on international politics for the re-establishment of religious unity, the treaties of Westphalia had shattered these illusions. The religious map of Europe was almost finally determined. England, the United Provinces, Scandinavia and Brandenburg, which was now to be reckoned with, henceforward had a Protestant policy. The position was all the more irreversible as the concept of the balance of power had banished the dream of a supranational authority, in which the Church might have had a part to play. Increasingly the nations were becoming conscious of their individuality and, under the absolute governments, which were in a majority, the State religions were giving birth to dangerous particularisms.

As regards the Church, it was in France, where absolutism was the most extreme, that it had to pay most dearly for what might be called patronage, in the worst sense of the word. To such a degree, indeed, that the word "Gallicanism" has been used to describe a similar state of affairs in other countries. The fact that Rome, in opposition to Jansenism, had need of all the help the king could give, served still more to enhance the latter's authority.

It must be remembered that this period showed none of the conformism that is sometimes imagined, and that to the grave crisis of Jansenism was added a strong free-thinking current among the upper classes and the bourgeoisie, and also, that a further crisis towards the end of the century, that of Quietism, was to cause division among the foremost members of the clergy. It can thus be well imagined that the fear of further estrangements was at all times a major anxiety of the Holy See. Although it was powerless in the temporal sphere, it at least took a firm stand in the doctrinal field, and defended its positions in the ecclesiastical world with great stubbornness.

It required the high qualities of Fabio Chigo, despite Mazarin's efforts elected pope in 1655, with the title of Alexander VII, simply to maintain the authority of the Church, especially as his predecessors, Sixtus V and Urban VIII in particular, had given to the Roman Congregations so much authority that there were limitations to papal initiative. This was just the period in France in which Jansenism was gaining support, while the Fronde, in which Retz and Mazarin were opposing one another, made the diplomatic game infinitely delicate. There were to be troubles of another kind, but still very grave ones, when the young Louis XIV, anxious to strengthen his prestige, insisted on a surrender painful to self-respect, in the matter of the Corsican guard (1662–4). There were difficulties in Spain about the nunciature, in Poland, in Germany, where the Emperor Frederick III compromised the Catholic cause by his excessive measures against the Protestants. The chief merit of Alexander VII is possibly the manner in which he clearly defined the position of the Church towards Jansenism. He was also a great builder, to whom Rome owes a large part of its magnificence.

Although the pontificate of Clement IX (1667–9) was short, it is important because of the lasting effect of the acts by this pope, who was very well informed on political matters and was conciliatory by nature. The formulary imposed on the Jansenists by his predecessor had split the episcopate into two parties. Clement preferred an appeasing vagueness, which for a time put an end to the conflict and enabled the Jansenists to place their qualities at the service of the battle against Protestantism. This "Clementine peace" lasted for thirty years.

Of Clement X (1670–6) it can be said that he followed the same policy, but Gallicanism, the Protestant question, and the Turkish danger—for Crete had fallen into the hands of the Turks in 1669—all called for a great pope, who arrived in the person of Innocent XI (1676–89). His firmness was accompanied by a very lively sense of reality. Thus, after approving the Revocation of the Edict of Nantes, he criticized the persecution which followed it and he deplored the blunders of James II in England. He took vigorous action against nepotism, Laxism and the errors of Molinos, the forerunner of Quietism. It is certain that with him, reform of the Church began afresh. He was aware that his struggle against an easy religion might lead to his being suspected of favouring Jansenism, and in the event, unjustly indeed, this is what happened. In dealing with Gallicanism below we shall see the bitterness of the struggle that ensued. He was also the pope who appealed for action against the Turks, and it was to him, as much as to Jean Sobieski, that the raising of the siege of Vienna (1683) and the liberation of Hungary were due, victories which are somewhat forgotten elsewhere than in Central Europe, but which are of no less importance than the battle of Poitiers.

Of Alexander VIII (1689–91) and of Innocent XII (1691–1700), it can be said that principally they reaped the harvest of the previous pontificate. The former is notorious for his nepotism, against which the latter reacted strongly. And if Innocent XII had the satisfaction of putting an end to the Gallican quarrel and of settling the question of Quietism, he witnessed the resurgence of Jansenism and, in the Far East, the revival of a pitiable rivalry between Dominicans and Jesuits over the Chinese rites.

Thus, at the dawn of the eighteenth century, the papacy seemed to be in a weakened state. In a world in which it was still futile to try and influence nations in order to preserve an ideal, and in which only despots and philosophers were of any account, the temporal unimportance of the popes left them disarmed in face of the former, while a declining spirituality served them badly against the latter. The many saints, which Rome itself sheltered at this period, changed nothing in this state of affairs.

CHAPTER VIII

RELIGIOUS THOUGHT, INSTITUTIONS AND LIFE

Too much has been said about the eighteenth century being a century of light. Such a remark means forgetting that this light was already shining, though possibly not so brightly, in earlier times, and that already the religious spirit was declining. This was true of the whole of Christendom. What was being witnessed, in general, was an acceleration of the movement caused by the Renaissance. Intellectual life, and life itself, grew apart from religion and became autonomous, and scientific progress seemed to be bound up with this independence. Religious wars had for a time arrested this evolution, and with some violence had caused man to turn his thoughts towards God. From this sprang the fine flower of the first half of the century. However, this very violence, by its useless continuance, together with the repugnance to forms of worship imposed by force, had developed the spirit of toleration, which was a good thing, but also indifference, which was not. The English thinkers, especially Locke, in his *Epistolae de Tolerantia* (1689–92), played a capital part in this movement. In France, Ninon de Lenclos and Saint-Evremond, who was an important link with English society, helped to spread this new spirit. This was strengthened by the evolution of Cartesianism, which was inclined to throw overboard everything which went beyond human understanding. With Fontenelle, and his *Entretiens sur la pluralité des mondes* (1686) and his *Histoire des Oracles* (1687); and Pierre Bayle, *Pensées sur la Comète* (1683) and especially his *Dictionnaire historique et critique*, the way was already marked out for Voltaire and the Encyclopedists.

The Church, at that time, was not short of defenders but leaders like those of the last century were no longer to be found. In France, in Italy and to a lesser degree in Germany, development of religious knowledge continued, the last stage, but a true continuation of the whole work inspired by the Council of Trent. The Bible had at this time in the person of the Oratorian, Richard Simon, an exegetist of the first rank, whose critical spirit was much in advance of that of his contemporaries, a fact which possibly made his condemnation expedient but certainly unjust. In apologetics, the great name is that of Bossuet, whose work, in contrast, was perfectly in keeping with the times: *Discours sur l'Histoire Universelle*; *Politique tirée de l'Écriture Sainte*, in which he defends the divine right of kings; and *Variations des Églises protestantes*. To these could be added the work of Daniel Huet, bishop of Avranches, and, in quite another manner, but with the permanent value given to it by genius, the *Pensées* of Pascal. The last name evokes also the polemics raised by questions of moral theology, and, if the extreme probabilism of an Escobar made this Jesuit too easy a target for the author of *Les Provinciales*, strangely enough, the regrettable outcome of this antagonism was to strengthen the position of the Jansenists.

It is most probably by its eloquent sermons, and by the names of Bossuet, Fénelon, Fléchier and Bourdaloue, that the religious aspect of the reign of Louis XIV is engraved on the memory of most people today, but it must be mentioned that this eloquence was at the service of the great men of the world and, at this same period, preachers in Germany and Italy, possibly in less perfect language, but moved by an admirable missionary spirit, were concerned with a much wider audience. Such was Abraham a Sancta Clara, a discalced Augustinian, who was a preacher at the emperor's court but who spoke also to the common people: such, too, were the Capuchin friar, Martin von Cochem, and Paul Segneri and Marco d'Aviano.

This picture of intellectual activity would not be complete without giving a prominent place to the historians, and, above all, to the French Congregation of the Benedictines of St Maur, among whom Mabillon and his pupil Ruinart not only revived hagiography, but, by their truly critical methods, laid the foundations of the auxiliary studies of history. To them should be added, Lenain de Tillemont and Du Cange, great workers also on the annals of the Church.

Were there not, then, more urgent tasks, even in the monastic orders? Armand de Rancé (1672–1700) thought so. He had left a life of luxury and intellectual triumph to live under the most austere discipline of St Bernard. Commendatory abbot of the Cistercian monastery of La Trappe, he reformed it and created the Order of Trappists, with a return to a life of asceticism and contemplation. He thus made his monastery one of the places where the Holy Spirit breathed and, to judge from the spectacle offered by many religious communities at that time, there was need for it. Rancé exerted such an attraction on souls eager for perfection that famous visitors, among them Bossuet on frequent occasions, came to make retreats with him. He might well have been canonized had not his severity led to his being accused of Jansenism. It should also be recalled with what intelligence Mabillon, in his *Traité des études monastiques*, in controversy with Rancé, defended the value of intellectual work performed in union with God, and with what subtlety he showed that to despise knowledge is a form of pride, when knowledge is such a great mistress of humility. Rancé had a follower in Eustace de Beaufort at Sept-Fons. In Germany the foundation of the

Congregation of Bavarian Benedictines also did much to raise the level of religious life.

The most original work, and certainly that with the widest social implications, was in education. A forerunner had been Charles Démia (1637–89), a priest who had been trained at Saint-Sulpice, who had created the "Little Schools", in the Lyons region, with a very modern system of pedagogy. At Rouen, also, a most meritorious attempt had been made by a Minim Friar, Nicolas Barré. The great success came in 1681 with the formation, by St John Baptist de La Salle, of the Brothers of the Christian Schools, who were to give an elementary education to the lower classes based on the French language. The workers and lower middle classes of the eighteenth century owed to this institution that moral health of which the upper did not always give an example.

A similar remark might be made about religious practice during the personal reign of Louis XIV. The truth is very complex and care must be taken not to generalize. The period of Fontenelle and of Bayle is also that in which devotion to the Sacred Heart revived piety in the world as it did in the monasteries. Not that this devotion was new, because it can also be found earlier among German mystics of the Middle Ages, and St John Eudes had also been its apostle. But it was a devotion completely rejuvenated by the visions of St Margaret Mary Alacoque between 1673 and 1675 at Paray-le-Monial and spread abroad by the Jesuit Fr de la Colombière, in spite of the bitter hostility of the Jansenists. It was also the moment when the cult of the Immaculate Conception became general and when the custom of the Month of Mary began in Italy. The historian would do well to make mention of the appearance of these devotions, even of the simplest of them, since this is a field in which feeling has just as rightful a place as reason.

CHAPTER IX

JANSENISM AND QUIETISM

In the life of the Church in the seventeenth century and in a large part of the eighteenth, there was no crisis more serious than that caused by Jansenism, especially in France. Cornelius Jansen, professor of theology at the University of Louvain, and later bishop of Ypres, left behind him, at his death in 1638, a book, the *Augustinus*, published two years later, in which, by an exaggerated interpretation of the thought of St Augustine, he came near to the Calvinist position. In his opinion man was irremediably corrupt owing to original sin, and could only be saved by grace granted by God to the predestined alone. This was to deny free will and to assert at the same time that Christ had not died to save all men. This harsh doctrine appeared in the full flood of the Catholic revival, at a moment when among laity and religious alike there was a strong reaction against a lax morality, and when, particularly in educated circles, the thirst for perfection was accompanied by a genuine love of austerity.

Jansen's teaching found passionate supporters, but at the same time it led to a religion of fear, one so exacting that it became almost impossible to receive communion. Its disheartening symbol became the so-called "Jansenist" crucifix whose arms were no longer open to all. The Church, already sorely tried by the Reformation, was obliged to intervene, and with the greater vigour because it was soon confronted by enterprising propagandists. One of these, in particular, was a friend of Jansen's, Jean Duvergier de Hauranne, commendatory abbot of Saint-Cyran, who was determined to transform religious life on the basis of the new doctrine. In 1641, the *Augustinus* was placed on the Index, a decision which Urban VIII upheld in the following year by the Bull *In Eminenti*.

In the opinion of those thus condemned, it was the teaching of St Augustine himself which was called in question. Actually, they were not unpowerful, for Saint-Cyran influenced the Cistercian nuns at the convent of Port-Royal, in Paris, where he was confessor, and their very remarkable abbess, Angélique Arnauld, together with the latter's brother, Antoine Arnauld, a theologian of great authority at the Sorbonne. Another centre of Jansenism was set up at Port-Royaldes-Champs, in the outer suburbs of Paris, the original seat of the abbey, where Mother Angélique had welcomed those who were called the "Solitaries" or the "Gentlemen of Port-Royal". These were men, both priests and laymen, who led there a life of work and prayer, keeping also small schools where they taught Latin and Greek. Racine was one of their pupils. They had great moral authority and their connections with the most select Paris society circles, particularly in the parliamentary world, strengthened their influence.

Against them stood principally the Jesuits, whose moral teaching was quite different. This antagonism became violent when Arnauld's book, *De la Communion fréquente*, appeared in 1643; it bristled with the obstacles it placed to approaching the Lord's Table. Arnauld, who now appeared as the spiritual leader of Jansenism, was increasingly influential. The majority of the episcopate then appealed to Rome for a decision on five propositions from the *Augustinus*. These propositions were condemned as heretical by the Bull of Innocent X, *Cum occasione*, in 1653. All the same, the question was not settled for the Jansenists, accepting the condemnation, denied that these five propositions appeared in Jansen's teaching and submitted that the infallibility of the Church, limited to matters of dogma, could not be invoked on this question of fact. Therefore, all that the Church could demand was a respectful silence. During the acute controversy which arose on this point Arnauld and many other doctors were excluded from the Sorbonne, but their chief opponents, the Jesuits, were the object of violent attacks on the ground of the laxity of their casuistry. The most dangerous attacks, owing to the authority and satirical genius of the author, were the *Provinciales* of Pascal (1656–7), whose sister was at Port-Royal. The book was put on the Index, and banned by the king, but it dealt such a blow to the Society of Jesus that it may be said that traces of it can still be seen.

Rome did not allow this equivocation by the Jansenists to continue. Alexander VII affirmed that the five propositions did form part of the doctrine of Jansen. In 1657 the General Assembly of the Clergy of France drew up a formulary of submission which, though it was approved by the pope, was not accepted by many Jansenists. At this juncture, the crisis took on a political aspect, for the king, whose personal rule was just beginning, considered that the Jansenists, among whom were many members of Parliament, had taken up common cause with a dangerous opposition party. In 1664, the archbishop of Paris, Hardouin de Péréfixe, placed an interdict on the Convent of Port-Royal and the nuns were dispersed. But there were, among the higher clergy, opponents less easy to subdue. The four bishops of Alet, Pamiers, Beauvans and Angers, the first two of whom were prelates of great worth, encouraged their clergy to adopt the attitude of respectful silence. The king, fearing both the popularity of these bishops and also the possible harmful effect on his authority if a sanction came from Rome, negotiated with the pope, who was no longer Alexander VII but Clement IX, a more diplomatic pontiff, who was very alarmed at the proportions assumed by the crisis. And so, in 1669, a settlement was reached, called the Clementine Peace, by which the bishops officially accepted the formulary but retained the right secretly to maintain their belief in the purity of the intentions of Jansen.

This artificial solution only made the evil dormant. Minds continued to be divided, and outside France, Jansenism made fresh conquests; thus it appeared in the Spanish Low Countries, whither Antoine Arnauld had fled for refuge, and still more so in the United Provinces, where practically the whole of the clergy, with the exception of the Jesuits, had gone over to the false doctrine. In France, what contributed to a prolongation of the truce was the Gallican quarrel, in which the bishops of Jansenist tendencies, hostile to the king, loyally served the cause of the Holy See.

However regrettable this Jansenist crisis, at least it proved that those who took part in it were not the indifferent. It is easy to have the defects of one's qualities, and it was because there were still in France very religious souls that there developed, at the moment when the Jansenist crisis was growing calmer, a pseudo-mystical movement, Quietism, against which in its turn the Church was obliged to fight.

The state of mind which it revealed was not new, nor could it be. It corresponds to a well-known type of behaviour, to one of those natural propensities to which it is dangerous to abandon oneself without control. This had been the case with the Illuminati, proceeded against by the Spanish Inquisition. God alone could say how many Quietists there were, in the shade of the cloisters, without being called by that name, and how many there still are. A praiseworthy form of Quietism was that of St Francis de Sales, who counselled abandonment in the arms of God but without losing thereby control of one's actions, nor becoming totally inactive. In this way he came near to stoicism, but giving it a Christian setting. This disturbing tendency came to light again with Molinos, a Spanish theologian, who lived in Rome after 1663. His theories went so far as to attract the pope, Innocent XI himself, at one period. In his *Spiritual Guide*, which appeared in 1675, Molinos put forward, as the ideal of the contemplative life, a condition in which the soul, now completely passive, annihilates itself before God. Carried to its extreme limits this doctrine makes vocal prayer and good works useless. It excludes even the idea of sin, since a soul so detached could not be held responsible for what, in outward appearance, would seem reprehensible.

This new mysticism spread very quickly, as much by the seductive influence of its mixture of idealism and facility, as by the great number of adherents Molinos had, and his extensive correspondence. Molinos' success proved his downfall. Arrested in 1689, he was brought before a board of inquiry, which revealed his immorality. Innocent XI censured the letters which had been published. Molinos, after recanting, was shut up in a monastery where he died in 1696.

But in the meantime Quietism had found a favourable soil in France. There its propagators were François Lacombe, a Barnabite, who, in his book *Analyse de l'Oraison mentale*, expounded theories close to those of Molinos, and, especially, a rich widow, Madame Guyon, enterprising and fanatical. Both of them were arrested, and, in 1694, a committee of theologians, gathered at Issy under the chairmanship of Bossuet, exposed the errors of Lacombe. The affair would have gone no further had not Fénelon, who admired and respected Madame Guyon, taken up her defence. In reply to Bossuet's *Instruction pastorale sur les états d'oraison*, appeared the *Explication des maximes des saints sur la vie intérieure* by Fénelon, the Archbishop of Cambrai. This controversy between the two most prominent prelates in France caused a sensation, especially as the king and Madame de Maintenon intervened against Fénelon. The lack of dignity with which Bossuet behaved towards his opponent lowered the reputation of that great figure, and it must be noted that the influence of Louis XIV played a great part in the condemnation of Fénelon's book by Innocent XII in 1699. Fénelon immediately submitted. Perhaps one day it will be known how great was the nobility implied in this act of obedience and silence. It may also be possible to discuss the assertion that the eighteenth century, with its revolutionary sentiments, may be the punishment for the persistent sympathy shown by Fénelon towards Guyonism. If that century sought for some satisfaction for the needs of its heart outside a religion in which to lose oneself in God was suspect, and thus came to lose itself in some other way, Bossuet played quite a definite part in this result.

CHAPTER X

GALLICANISM

In chapter I we saw the various aspects of Gallicanism before the first half of the seventeenth century and the grave problems raised by this movement. It is obvious that this trend could only be strengthened by such absolute power as that of Louis XIV, who found it hard to tolerate the authority which Rome had been able to keep over the clergy. In this he was ably seconded by a parliament which, in this respect, gave full vent to its long-standing hostility towards clerical jurisdiction, and also a higher clergy more or less subservient since the Concordat of 1516. Finally, he was helped by the Jansenists, although he was far from seeking their help; in fact quite the reverse.

At the beginning of his personal reign, a very significant incident occurred. In December, 1661, Fr Coret, a Jesuit, defended a thesis in the Sorbonne affirming papal infallibility in matters of fact as well as in dogma. If this thesis was timely in its opposition to Jansenism, it also supplied, perhaps deliberately, a weapon against Gallicanism. On this point the king was so sensitive, that, in spite of all his antipathy towards the Jansenists, he wished to take action against the Jesuit. It was with great difficulty that his confessor, Fr Annat, and the archbishop of Paris, de Marca, persuaded him to give up this idea.

In the following year, an unfortunate incident, during which some Corsicans in the pontifical guard killed a page from the retinue of the French ambassador, gave the king an opportunity of displaying all his pride and certain prelates the chance to show their servility.

Five months later, a further thesis at the Sorbonne, that of Drouet de Villeneuve, defending quite prudently the infallibility and authority of the pope, let loose Gallicans and Jansenists. If the king found it prudent not to follow Parliament in hostility towards the Sorbonne, wounds were reopened and hatred was alive.

It was in this atmosphere that the very grave matter of the Regale arose. The right of Regale was the one by which the king of France was entitled to the income from vacant bishoprics (temporal Regale) and to make nomination to the livings dependent on them (spiritual Regale), until such time as a new titular had taken the oath of allegiance. The temporal Regale had been admitted by the Holy See, but the second one, which raised very serious questions, was subject to qualification and did not apply to all dioceses. In February, 1673, the king decided that it would be applied throughout the whole of France, but he encountered the opposition of the bishops of Alet and Pamiers, who had already shown their Jansenist obstinacy, but this time they appealed to Rome; the pope condemned the measures which had been taken, as an improper intervention of the civil power into ecclesiastical matters and threatened to use the weapons he had at his disposal. This attitude exasperated the king, who knew that he would be able to rely on most of the higher clergy. Indeed, the house of Clergy of 1680 disapproved of the attitude of the pope, and, in the following year, a further meeting took place with a programme which almost made it a National Council. It was dominated by the personality of Bossuet, a Gallican completely devoted to the king, but conscious of the catastrophe that a break with Rome would be. He made a conciliatory speech on the unity of the Church, and managed to obtain a declaration confirming the right of Louis XIV, but, at the same time, taking away all real right in the spiritual field. This result did not satisfy the king who, overcoming the scruples of Bossuet, got him to draw up the famous *Déclaration des quatre articles* of 1682. The first of these affirmed the independence of the king in the temporal sphere: the second proclaimed the superiority of General Councils over the pope: the third proclaimed the respect due by the latter to Gallican usages, and, finally, the fourth stated the necessity for obtaining the consent of all the Churches before pontifical definitions in matters of faith could be held to be irrevocable. The greatest danger, that is, an actual appeal to a Council, was at least avoided.

The king wished to make the four articles, as has been said, into a "Gallican Creed". He insisted on it being taught, and made it obligatory for every candidate for a theological degree to subscribe to it. But some of the clergy protested, and Innocent XI, denying that the Declaration had any value, refused to install any signatories whom the king might nominate to vacant bishoprics. The king insisted and nominated to further sees for which the pope still refused to invest; rapidly the point was reached where 35 bishoprics were without incumbents. Relations were further strained in 1687 over a question of the right to asylum in the French Embassy in Rome (the right of sanctuary affair), and at one moment Louis XIV was even excommunicated, without it being made public however, and without his giving way. It was only in 1693, and after the death of Innocent XI, that negotiations ended in a compromise, which was, in reality, a defeat for the king. It was agreed that the four articles should no longer be taught, but the temporal prerogative was extended to all the dioceses. If the king gave way, it was because the matter would otherwise have led to a schism, and it was plain to see that the vast majority of the clergy would not have followed him in that.

CHAPTER XI

THE PROTESTANT

CHALLENGE

The Church is the body of all Christians subject to the pope but it would not be Christian, that is, faithful to Christ's teachings, if it did not seek to gather all men into one flock under a single shepherd. In the seventeenth century, it was particularly concerned with achieving this end in regard to the Protestants, separated brethren of recent date. Certain forms of Protestantism remained so near to Catholic spirituality that it looked as if the barriers might easily be overcome. It could also be considered, that in those regions where the rulers decided on the religion to be adopted, adherence to an enforced faith lacked any firm conviction.

From the Protestant side as well, there were certain attempts towards reunion, especially after the end of the Thirty Years War. Even before the war had finished, a professor of theology in the University of Helmstedt, in the Duchy of Brunswick, was seeking reconciliation; this was Georg Callisen (1586–1656), known as Calixtus. A great traveller, he had that open-mindedness which comes from varied contacts, and in his long study of the doctrine of the first five centuries, he had found elements favourable to reunion, which were worthy of being taken into consideration by the Eastern Church as well. It is hardly necessary to say that in matters such as this, it is the spirit which is important, as it is necessary to emphasize what unites and not what divides.

Unfortunately, this was not the opinion of his co-religionists, for whom already the differences between Lutheranism and Calvinism had become fundamental. At the Conference of Thorn (1645), he was accused of syncretism, that is, of wishing to unite incompatible doctrines, and he was attacked with great violence. The controversy aroused by his initiative lasted for half a century, and, even if many of these disputes did not rise above the level of petty squabbles, a path had been opened up towards greater understanding. Thus, Christian de Schönborn, archbishop of Mainz, was able to organize conferences with the professors of Helmstedt, and it was with a follower of Calixtus, namely Molanus, Protestant pastor of Lokkum, that the Spanish prelate, Christopher de Rojas y Spinola, bishop of Wiener-Neustadt, was in correspondence, in which the emperor on the one side and the Elector of Hanover on the other showed the greatest interest.

It was at this time that Leibniz was carrying on a correspondence with Bossuet, in which he showed his uprightness and his passionate wish to find a logical solution to these illogical divergences, since truth is indivisible. It was a moving dialogue but it was difficult for it to produce any definite result, as the French theologian based his argument mainly on historical grounds. To Bossuet's *Histoire des variations des Églises protestantes*, Pastor Jurieu replied by saying that the original Christian doctrine had itself varied "not only in form but in substance". When Bossuet quoted the unanimous agreement of all Catholics with the truths laid down at the Council of Trent, it must be admitted that the reformers were quite fair in using the same arguments against the infallibility of the Council as Bossuet had himself used in the Gallican dispute against the infallibility of the pope.

It can be conceived that, in a divided Germany, the return to the unity of the faith might have seemed desirable from the national point of view itself, and this consideration may have inspired efforts towards it, but great minds were considering the matter on a universal scale. This explains how, in the first half of the century, the famous Dutch lawyer, Hugo Grotius, founder of international law, had dreams not only of a harmonious league of Christian nations, but also of a common faith, as described in his *De veritate religionis christianae*.

Finally, there was a large number of conversions which were purely individual affairs, and these testify to the strong attraction which Catholicism still exerted. The example of Duke John of Hanover can be mentioned, a convert who made no claim to be able to bring his subjects with him; in fact he would have been firmly prevented from doing so. Also that of Johannes Scheffler, an attractive personality, a Protestant Silesian doctor of medicine, who became a Catholic priest and published, under the name of Angelus Silesius, maxims and poetry of great distinction, in which can be found inspiration from Tauler and Ruysbroek, with an idealism closely approaching Quietism, in a country where no one had any personal interest in being alarmed by it. Outside Germany, the conversion which attracted the greatest attention was that of Queen Christina of Sweden, daughter of that deceased great champion of the Reformation, Gustavus Adolphus. This, it must be said, was quite an isolated conversion in a Scandinavia which was strictly barred to missionaries.

In the second half of the century, however, Rome appointed vicars apostolic for the very small flock which was beginning to be tolerated there. The most famous of these was the Danish savant, Niels Steensen (1638–86), a convert, well known to doctors and naturalists, but of whose heroic efforts few Christians are aware.

There is no doubt that many of these conversions to Catholicism were inspired by the disputes between the Protestant Churches, by the cold austerity of their worship, as compared with the more friendly externals of the Roman Church, and, without stating any paradox, by the varied schools of spirituality which the latter offered without compromising thereby the unity of the faith. In the heart of Protestantism, another solution was offered, that of an evolution towards a more personal religion, with a deeper inner life, and a return to the loving charity of the first Christians. Such was the origin of Pietism.

Moreover, in the very earliest days of Protestantism the tendency was to be found in Schwenkfeld (1489–1561) and in those followers of Tauler and of Suso, the gentle and brotherly mystics in the Low Countries and in England. At the beginning of the seventeeth century this movement had found a supporter of very humble origin, Jacob Boehme (1575–1624), whose simple soul rose to the loftiest inspirations. In his many works, of which the best known is *Der Weg zu Christo* ("The Way to Christ"), there is to be found, alongside *simpliste* ideas expressed with the assurance of a visionary, a philosophy deep enough to have influenced Schelling and Hegel, with a strange poetry, which influenced German romanticism.

His contemporary, Johann Arndt (1555–1621), although less remarkable, probably had a still greater influence because of that fact. With a soul filled with love, he had retained, from his wide religious knowledge, all that he found congenial, and in simple but compelling words, he won hearts to a life of union with God in humility and brotherly love. He followed Luther, who was for him a Father of the Church, in his dogma of predestination but his religious belief is so close to Catholicism that a Latin translation of his chef d'oeuvre *Vier Bücher vom wahren Christentum* ("Four Books of True Christianity") could be published, without the author's name, and used by Catholics. It has been said that no other human work, other than the *Imitation*, has been reprinted so often.

With the coming of the Thirty Years War, there could be no question of any spiritual progress in a ravaged Germany. But the work of Arndt lived on after him. His "True Christianity" was one of the bedside books of that cultured Alsatian, Philip Jacques Spener (1635–1705), who was influenced also by the mystics of the fourteenth century, such as Tauler. Filled with charity like Arndt, he had possessed the additional advantage that he was an organizer. Having become chief Pastor in Frankfort-am-Main, where he had won over the lower classes by his kindness, he set up there an efficient system of elementary religious instruction, as well as classes both for the faithful and their pastors. In 1675, there appeared, under the title of *Pia desideria*, a whole programme for the improvement of religious studies, of missionary work and of the adaptation of the Christian life to the teachings of the Scriptures. This caused quite a sensation. His scheme provided for lay associations, called *Collegia pietatis*, and clerical associations, *Collegia philobiblion*, which quickly grew in numbers. He was attacked vindictively by the Lutherans and, after having lived in a number of towns, died in Berlin. He had given to Pietism its purest form and brought it to the highest point of its development. After him, pastors with too eccentric ideas, or of doubtful moral worth, did harm to the still very meritorious work of more sober disciples, and Pietism lived on, mainly in the elements which other sects borrowed from it. From the life of this great Christian there remained a new atmosphere among Protestants in Germany; despite his enemies, spiritual teaching in that country probably owes more to him than to Luther. A Catholic can do no other than pay respect to his memory, with the thought that God will surely have opened his arms to the servant who, with such great zeal and love, had worked on one of his vines, although it may not have been given its true name.

Spener's especial efforts—and it was this which aroused the great opposition—were directed to the unity of Protestantism.

This was also the aim of Leibniz if total Christian unity could not be achieved. The failure of both of them was no help to the Church for, apart from the thoughts provoked by Protestant division, Protestants were still solidly united against Rome. From these divisions grew indifference and agnosticism which caused the Germanic world to contribute very greatly to the rise of irreligion.

Much the same can be said about the British Isles, in spite of the fact that matters developed there in a totally different way. Under the dictatorship of Cromwell, the Puritans (the Independents) had crushed popery, Episcopalianism, and Presbyterianism. At the Restoration, a reaction against Puritanism and its excesses brought back the Anglican Church to its place. Charles II, in spite of his secret leanings towards Catholicism, could do no other than subscribe to the maintenance of Protestantism, in the form given to it by more than a hundred years of Tudor or Stuart kings. Unfortunately for the Catholics an unfortunate foreign policy seemed to make Catholicism the sign of subjection to foreign interests. As had been the case with the Gunpowder Plot in 1605, the Great Fire of London (1666), for which Catholics were certainly not responsible, was used against them and they were more than ever the subject of discriminating legislation. The best known of these laws was the Test Act, which compelled all holders of any public office to sign a declaration denying transubstantiation. In this way the king's brother, the Duke of York, was forced to give up his appointment of Lord High Admiral, and it was hoped to prevent him from succeeding Charles II.

There was a further piece of trickery in 1678, when Titus Oates, an Anglican minister dismissed by his Church for depraved living, laid information about a supposed Catholic plot, which was to include nothing less than the burning of London, a French invasion and a government set up by the Jesuits. Parliament pretended to believe this, and popular fury was let loose against the Catholics. The assassination of Sir Edmund Godfrey, one of the magistrates chosen to investigate this matter, was also blamed on the Catholics. The result was the execution of a number of priests and the death in prison of many more, together with the exclusion of Catholic peers from Parliament.

The question of the succession to the throne remained very much to the fore and caused a deep division in the country. At that time there was no party in the sense in which that term is now understood, but it can still be considered that there was a Tory, loyalist view which accepted the ordinary working of the law of succession, and consequently, a Catholic king, which the Duke of York looked like becoming; there was also a Whig view, which was opposed to any such event taking place. The blunders of the Whigs and the skilful policy of Charles II ensured that his brother could succeed him in 1685, with the title of James II.

Unfortunately the policy of James II was very clumsy. The punishment meted out to Titus Oates, which was certainly not illegal, and the measures taken to repair as far as possible the damage caused by this adventurer, provoked an unfortunate atmosphere of reaction. This feeling was still further strengthened by the appointment of Catholics to important positions, despite the Test Act. The king then attempted to have that Act, as well as the Habeas Corpus Act, repealed. He kept an unusually large number of troops near London and this may have given rise to the fear of a policy backed by military force. Finally, a Declaration of Indulgence, suspending the legislation preventing Catholics and Nonconformists holding office, increased this uneasiness still more, as did the sending of an ambassador to Rome, and the reception of a papal nuncio at Windsor. Innocent XI himself was not without misgivings about these new arrangements and advised prudence, and especially respect for parliamentary liberties. But there was another influence acting in the opposite direction; Louis XIV was urging the king of England towards a Catholic, absolutist reaction as a matter of principle in the first place, and also to further his own interests. He calculated, indeed, that the obstacles encountered by James II would make the latter his dependent. The harm done to the Catholic cause in England by these two monarchs was incalculable: Protestantism seemed to the English the best guarantee of their civil rights, and Catholicism was identified in their minds with absolute monarchy and foreign interference.

In 1688, a second Declaration of Indulgence, which was ordered to be read in the churches, provoked a serious conflict with the clergy, the arrest of seven Anglican bishops, who were acquitted amid general rejoicing, and anti-popery riots. The atmosphere was already very threatening when the birth of a Prince of Wales put an end to all hope of a Protestant succession. For until then the succession would have gone to Mary, the Protestant daughter of the first marriage of James II to a Protestant; she was the wife of William of Orange, Stadholder of Orange. The Revolution of 1688 placed William and Mary on the throne, after guarantees of public liberties had been obtained from them as also for the Protestant religion and for effective control by Parliament. The early years of William had not prepared him for any particular sympathy with the Anglican High Church, as his inclination was to put Anglicans and Nonconformists on the same level and he was not ill-disposed towards Catholics. An Act of Tolerance gave a large measure of freedom to the Nonconformists, but still they were not admitted to sit in Parliament, nor to hold high office. But the Catholics did not benefit from this Act. Still suspect, they were deprived of political rights and even of some civil rights, such as that of making a will in favour of other Catholics. Public services of the Catholic religion were forbidden, in principle, and priests were prosecuted. Actually, there was a movement towards toleration, even to indifference, and these draconian laws were applied to a lessening degree. Nevertheless, Great Britain was to wait until the nineteenth century before there was a considerable Catholic revival.

Apart from its detestation of the power of Rome, the Church of England was not so very far removed from the Catholic Church, and the High Church, in particular claimed that it still remained part of the Church. But from the Low Church, much closer to Calvinism, down to the Levellers, that is the rationalists, and to the Diggers, or landworkers, dreaming of a communal Christian community, the proliferation of sects can be explained as much by unsatisfied aspirations as by a large measure of liberty. This freedom was denied for a long time in England to the Quakers, whose founder was George Fox (1624–90). This was because his doctrine rejected all organization, sacrament and priest, and even scorned any place of worship, so as to give value to the practice of virtue alone, to the inner life and to the enlightenment of the soul by God. In their silent meetings, their adherents waited for this inspiration to reveal itself to one or to another by spiritual trembling, whence the name given to them in mockery, which they made their banner. There was a large element of subjectivity in a religion so conceived and the activities of this sect in its early days were often strange and noisy. But the Society of Friends, as the Quakers called themselves, got rid of its peculiarities very quickly, and it was the ideals of honesty and fraternity of its founder which gave it its distinguishing mark. Persecuted in England, the Quakers prospered in America, where William Penn, protected by Charles II, went to found the State of Pennsylvania and its capital, Philadelphia, the city of brotherly love. It must be recognized that, on the whole, the adherents of this religion, which was largely a system of morality, did a great deal of good.

Unfortunately, the same cannot be said of the English, whether Anglicans or Independents, with whom Catholic

Ireland had to deal. Charles II did no more than Charles I to improve the lot of this island. The hopes placed by the Irish on James II were soon destroyed by the Revolution of 1688, and that ruler completed their misfortune by relying on them to reconquer his crown for him. After the Battle of the Boyne (1690) where the Stuart king was defeated, the Treaty of Limerick made Ireland a veritable English colony, in which Catholics were subjected to iniquitous conditions.

Excesses of this kind double the appreciation felt for the work for peace accomplished in France by the Edict of Nantes. In all fairness, it must be acknowledged that in Ireland the antagonism was national at least as much as it was religious, and that the union among Catholics was a great trouble to the English. In France, where the position of the Church in relation to a definite minority of Protestants made concessions possible, it was also largely on the political side that the most serious problems arose. The Edict of Nantes had given the Protestants a definite political status, from which they sought to gain some advantage, and the State within a State, which they had finally managed to set up, made the use of military measures essential, of which the siege of La Rochelle was the outstanding episode. The Edict, called the Peace of Alais (1629), had given full religious liberty to the reformers, but took away their right to hold assemblies and to raise taxes. Richelieu, having obtained these guarantees, showed himself remarkably benevolent, being anxious that the Protestants should not feel they were lower-grade citizens, and avoided any semblance of proselytism, which would have been impolitic. Mazarin also showed in this matter the discretion which could be expected from so able a politician, and the result was that, in the middle of the century, many Protestants were important and honoured personages, some of them attaining to the highest civil or military posts.

Richelieu excellently defined the proper attitude from the Catholic point of view when he said to Louis XIII: "I have only sought to remove faction from among your subjects. Anything more than that is the work of heaven and this we must wait for, without bringing to bear any other violence than by leading a good life and showing a good example."

Louis XIV was unable to maintain this wise policy. He belonged to another generation, no longer aware of certain realities, which shared the error of the king. But it was primarily the conditions accompanying his birth and education, in which his mother, brought up in the Spanish tradition, laid special emphasis on the instruction he was already receiving about the divine right of kings, and also his desire to perfect the unity of his kingdom, which led him towards a solution imposed by force. He was also driven in that direction by the clergy, a point which has possibly not been sufficiently emphasized. Surprise is sometimes expressed at the fact that some recent converts from Protestantism, such as Pellisson and especially Madame de Maintenon, used their influence in the same direction, but this would be to forget the zeal often shown by converts. Finally, there were the political considerations, namely, the opposition of Holland, the home of Protestantism, to the conquests of Louis XIV, and also the suspicion that the French Calvinists were in fact or in spirit conniving with their coreligionists in the United Provinces.

This is not the place to recall in what manner, after somewhat vain attempts to use persuasion and then intimidation, recourse was had to violent methods, of which the best known are the dragooning and sentencing to the galleys of the Huguenots. Nor is it here that there should be enumerated the irreparable losses, both intellectual and economic, which were the result of extensive emigration. When biased reports had persuaded the king of the effectiveness of these methods, it was easy to convince him that the suppression of the reformed religion could be achieved and the final resistance overcome "without its costing one further drop of blood".

Most certainly it was also a pleasure for Louis XIV to prove to the pope, by striking a great blow against this heresy, that the Gallican king who had so injured him was still a very Christian king.

The Edict revoking the Edict of Nantes was signed therefore on October 18th, 1685. It now appears to us as one of the gravest mistakes in French history. Emigration reached tremendous proportions but this was only possible for the rich. The poor had to stay. This was the heroic period of the meetings in lonely places, of the "Camisards" (the White-Shirts) when repression was sometimes so merciless that some Catholic prelates protested and Innocent X was upset by it.

The material losses suffered by France from this emigration seem to have been exaggerated sometimes, but this cannot be said about the moral harm done to the country by the Revocation and by the violent measures which accompanied it. In the eyes of the other nations, France was a country of the most brutal intolerance. Catholicism lost even more, as its opponents could assert that these methods, so contrary to the Christian spirit, were the usual methods of Catholicism. At the same time many of the faithful themselves, from the king downwards, were leading lives which did little honour to their religion.

On the other hand, Protestantism benefited from the sympathy which is always shown towards the persecuted, and from all the philosophical and moral authority given to their faith by those who defend it to the death. And, finally, how great was the propaganda done by the emigrants outside France!

When the facts are carefully examined, it will be found that it was not only Catholicism which suffered but the idea of Christianity itself. In a world in which religious conflicts were becoming less brutal, it looked as if crimes could once again be committed in the name of Christ against human liberty and simple charity. It can be clearly seen, in the closing years of the seventeenth century, how great was the support given to the arguments for Deism by these religious conflicts, and how much rationalism also gained from them.

CHAPTER XII

CATHOLIC EXPANSION THROUGHOUT THE WORLD

It might be imagined that the simple wish to be symmetrical in dealing with the missionary work of the Church would justify the division made here between the first and the second half of the seventeenth century. Certainly, when it is a question of subject-matter as complex and interwoven as history, there is always something artificial about a plan, essential though it may be. It must, however, be recognized that, towards the middle of the century, in 1659 to be exact, there occurs a document of the greatest importance, which makes it essential to take bearings and then to define the spirit and coordinate the methods by which missionary work was accomplished. This document is the instructions given by the Congregation for the Propagation of the Faith to the vicars apostolic. And the vicars apostolic, who date from this same period, are bishops dependent on the Holy See alone and charged with the duty of establishing a native clergy.

It has been seen, earlier, what conflicts placed the religious Orders in opposition to one another in the first half of the century on the subject of missionary methods. For one side, everything was to be rejected which savoured of pagan customs, both in manner of life and beliefs, and for them were to be substituted all the externals associated with the Christian Faith in Europe. It was with great reluctance that they even agreed to the admission of native clergy. For the opposite side, it was a question of proving to the peoples outside Europe that the God of the Christians was not the God of one race only, but that his worship could be taken into their normal way of living, and could be taught to them in their own language, and that apostles would be found from among them. Experience had shown the effectiveness of the second method and it was this pattern which the 1659 instructions recommended. Not that it was necessary to retain all heathen customs, for not all of them were compatible with Christian faith and ethics, but, even in such cases, these must be progressively replaced, as understanding and a sense of proportion were essential to success.

This document, full of charity and understanding, marked an epoch, but unfortunately it was far from being generally applied. In China, for instance, rivalry between the religious Orders broke out again, thus compromising the brilliant results already achieved. This was especially kept alive by the custom of converts continuing to offer sacrifices to ancestors and to Confucius. Everything depends upon the spirit with which these rites were conducted. They could have been no more incompatible with the Christian faith than are prayers for the dead in our country, but it was imperative for the Church to remove any possibility of ambiguity on this point. This was done by a decision of Clement XI, condemning these rites in 1704. The pontifical legate, entrusted with the duty of notifying the emperor of this ruling, did it in an undiplomatic manner and was arrested. The Jesuits only submitted to this interdiction at a much later date, while the other Orders, the Dominicans particularly, continued their opposition. This was a great evil for the missions, and the decline of Christianity soon became evident.

In South America, where a Jesuit, Fr Anchieta, had already

done so much for the evangelization of Brazil, it was again a Jesuit, Fr Antonio de Vieira (1608–97), who played the most important part. Gifted with high intellectual qualities, and having proved his worth in Portugal and in the embassy entrusted to him, he devoted his life, after 1652, to the evangelization of the savages in Brazil, north of the Amazon. As he snatched Indians from slavery and defended them against the settlers, he was the victim of the latter's vengeance, arrested, and even condemned by the Holy See for doing what was subsequently recognized as blameless. Released, and loaded with honours, he died in Brazil, after having carried out a work which, thanks to his understanding of the native mentality, can still serve as a model.

But it was particularly in North America that the most powerful Christian communities were set up, as there it was not so much a question of missions to the natives but rather that of settlements of Europeans who were already believers, or of the taking in hand again of various groups, settlers, fishermen or trappers, whose religious practice had greatly declined.

Thus, in 1658, Margaret Bourgeoise founded the Congregation of Notre-Dame in the growing city of Montreal which soon became, by the efforts of the Sulpicians, the second centre in Canada. The following year saw the arrival of the Vincentians, to whom Mgr de Montigny-Laval, at first vicar apostolic and then bishop of Quebec, entrusted the seminary, the nucleus of the future University of Laval, and also a college.

In Nova Scotia also, there was great missionary activity which contributed to the maintenance of Catholicism in a region destined to suffer tragic days during the following century.

The missions met with great resistance from the natives, due largely to the attachment of the Indians to habits of life far removed from Christian morality. Many were the priests who paid with their lives for a thankless apostolate.

PART III

THE CENTURY OF LIGHT: THE CHURCH AND RATIONALISM

As "the child is father of the man," so do the essential features of the eighteenth century make themselves clearly visible from about 1680. The dates which Paul Hazard fixed for his book, *The European Mind* (London, 1953), namely 1680 to 1715, agree closely with this. Fundamentally, even in France, the period of undisputed power, of conformism, of assurance, which is too widely taken as the hallmark of the century, did not, on a final analysis, last twenty years, and the next century was already taking shape. In the new century, absolutism generally persists, but under an external appearance of philosophy which, from the spiritual point of view with which this book is concerned, is infinitely more harmful. The Church suffered from it the more since it was accompanied by the rise of two monarchies separated from Rome, those of Prussia and Russia. Meanwhile, in Catholic Austria, governmental interference in religious matters took the extreme form which was called Josephism. This phenomenon showed itself also, in varying degrees, in the Bourbon kingdoms. The suppression of the Jesuits, forced on Rome, is one of the most striking examples of this interference. But all these countries pale before England, a Protestant power whose influence was growing in Europe and outside it.

However hazardous the position appeared by the extent of the influence of the temporal power on the spiritual, the outlook was still more threatening in the purely religious sphere. Indeed, unorthodox doctrines, like Jansenism or Febronianism, continued to give great anxiety, but to these must be added Deistic and rationalistic movements, which made headway throughout the century. It can be said that the preceding century, even with all its religious divisions, had remained Christian. The eighteenth century became less and less so. It would be easy, by going back to humanism, to Cartesianism and to the free-thinkers, to demonstrate the source of this evolution. It was hastened by scientific progress and by a tendency to look to science for the solution of all problems, and also by a misunderstood spirit of toleration, in the sense that in a desire for peace truth went by the board. Finally account must be taken of the whole movement of anti-Christian philosophy spread abroad by the learned societies. Resignation of the leading men and a crisis in the government, in addition to all these factors, explain the sequel: the "century of light" ended in the Revolution. This occurred first in France but the revolutionary spirit was growing elsewhere and was contagious in the particular field covered by this book. There is no question of denying its constructive benefits and it cannot be questioned that it brought to the world a great ideal of social justice and certain freedoms. But here it must be pointed out that directly from the religious point of view it was a catastrophe.

CHAPTER XIII

CHURCH GOVERNMENT

Already in the period which, by general consent, is called the Renaissance, and with the rise of Humanism, the Church had met with dangers comparable with those which the century of light had brought to it. But, if too many of the Renaissance popes had bowed down to the spirit of paganism and even indulged in its vices too obviously, those of the eighteenth century, in spite of their reduced political power, were worthy and sometimes admirable upholders of Christian doctrine and traditions. Of noble origin for the most part, and in many cases with diplomatic experience before arriving at the supreme pontificate, they played a singularly difficult part, if it can be so described, by giving way at times on minor details to make sure of saving the essentials. If they are not very well known, except for the latest of them, that is because, for the later popes, it was a time of great cataclysms whereas, for the earlier ones, it had been a time of growing underground danger. Furthermore, they were no longer sovereigns of any account in temporal matters, and the moment had not yet arrived when great social and doctrinal teaching was to bring their successors into prominence.

It can truly be said that Clement XI (1700–21), the first pope of the period now being considered, experienced the most typical of the difficulties encountered by the Church during this century, and not only at their early stage but already in formidable shape. His efforts against Jansenism—

his Bull *Unigenitus* (1713) is the most famous example—did not prevent its development in France, nor its propagation in Holland and Italy. This evolution which, among certain groups was to go so far as schism, coincided, unfortunately, with a rapid rise of the new philosophy. Outside Europe, the pope had the sorrow of seeing the Maronites break away from Rome, and of the increasing bitterness of the quarrels about the Chinese rites. In his relations with the various Powers, Clement XI was not any happier. At the beginning of his pontificate, he saw the Emperor, in spite of papal protestations, allow the Elector of Brandenburg to take the title of King of Prussia, thus giving increased prestige to a Protestant monarchy. Within less than half a century, Catholic Austria was fated to suffer the consequences of this weakness. However, in Poland, Clement XI had the satisfaction of seeing, after many vicissitudes, the triumph of his candidate, Frederick Augustus II, over the candidate of Charles XII, Stanislas Leczinski. But it was only a relative triumph, as it was Russian influence which dominated Poland under Augustus II. In the War of the Spanish Succession, the pope's position was a difficult one, and his relations with Emperor Joseph I became strained, while the papal nuncio was expelled from Madrid and all communication between the Spanish bishops and Rome was forbidden. Finally, there was the break with Victor Amadeus II of Savoy, owing to the pope's refusal to recognize him as king of Sicily.

It is also during the short pontificate of Innocent XIII (1721–4) that it can be seen to what an extent the great Catholic Powers pressed heavily on the Church. His election itself had been made under the *exclusive*, that is the right which the rulers of Spain, France and Austria had arrogated to themselves for centuries past to exercise their veto against the election of a pope who was not acceptable to them. Innocent XIII profited by an intervention of this kind by the emperor and probably more so by the French government and it is

still a debatable question whether the latter had not previously obtained from the future pope an undertaking to relax
his opposition to Jansenism and also to raise the notorious
Abbé Dubois to the cardinalate. This actually took place but,
in view of the pressure put upon him, one is reluctant to
accuse a worthy and loving pastor of weakness, as he probably
thought that by so doing he was preventing still greater evils.

Similarly, Benedict XIII (1724–30), an eminent thinker who
was looked upon as a saint by those near to him, was unable
effectively to oppose the interference of Catholic rulers in
ecclesiastical affairs. It is true that he was badly served by a
despicable adviser, Cardinal Coscia, and by his Secretary of
State, Cardinal Lercari. But he was very clever in finding
appeasing formulas, which resulted in the Bull *Unigenitus*
being accepted in France, and his great moral authority
enabled him to impose on the clergy a closer regard for their
duties.

In the same way, Clement XII (1730–40) was forced to
allow the rulers of the House of Bourbon, who shared Latin
Europe among them, to encroach on his prerogatives. In
addition to the disappointment caused by being compelled to
give way before the temporal power of those who ought to
have been the most faithful supporters of the Church, the
pope had the additional distress of witnessing the rise of the
great non-Catholic powers, as previously mentioned. It was in
1738 that Clement XII issued his Bull, *In Eminenti*, against
Freemasonry, which was playing such an important part in
propagating the new philosophy. By its secret meetings at
which men of the most divergent beliefs were drawn together,
it was a great menace to the Faith.

If there was one pope of the eighteenth century who gave
the impression of being open to the ideas of his time, that
pope was Benedict XIV (1740–58). Very cultured, "enlightened" would be the proper word, and good-natured, so that he
was very popular, his policy was one of moderation which

led to his being charged with weakness. On the questions of Portugal, the Two Sicilies and the King of Prussia, he willingly granted concessions for the sake of cordial relations, whereas it would have been necessary to drag them out of his predecessors. By advising the Congregation of the Index to use moderation and discretion in the application of the Bull *Unigenitus*, he gained the sympathetic respect of the Protestants. An English peer said that "If he came to London, he would make us all papists". He carried on a correspondence with Frederick II, and Voltaire dedicated his *Mahomet* to him. It would be a mistake, however, to attribute to laxity, what was nothing but charity and good diplomacy. This pope treated serious questions with gravity, and by renewing the condemnation of freemasonry, by condemning a book which portrayed him as being favourably inclined towards Jansenism, and by condemning an edition of Voltaire's Works, he clearly defined the limits which were not to be crossed.

The personality of this man of peace served only to put off the coming storms. This was already felt in the Conclave summoned for the election of his successor, when a French cardinal supporting the policies of the Bourbon courts, pronounced a veto against a member of the Sacred College who had every prospect of being elected but who was known to be favourable towards the Jesuits. Obstinate defenders of the authority and of the prerogatives of the Holy See, the Jesuits, for this very reason, were the object of the hostility of those Catholic rulers, especially of the Bourbons, who were seeking an increasing control of their clergy. In France, the Jesuits had against them the members of Parliament, constant supporters of the theories of Gallicanism, as well as the Jansenists and, obviously, the philosophers.

The pope who was elected under these conditions, was a saintly priest, Clement XIII (1758–69), whose first measures were intended to recall the episcopacy to the greatness of its responsibilities. He had not long to wait before realizing that years of conflict were opening before him. At the very beginning of his pontificate, there was an attempt on the life of the king of Portugal which served as a pretext for the Prime Minister, Pombal, to throw suspicion on the Jesuits and get them expelled. In 1762, Choiseul succeeded in getting the Parliament of Paris to suppress the Society of Jesus in its jurisdiction, and the Provincial Parliaments did the same. Spain followed in 1767, Parma in 1768. Clement XIII had hoped that Maria Theresa, whom he had honoured with the title of "Her Apostolic Majesty", would intervene, but he was disappointed, and this formed only the beginning of the disillusion which increasingly he suffered at the hands of Joseph II.

The attacks on the Jesuits were only the preliminary skirmishes of a great offensive. In France, as in Germany, the ruling bodies interfered more and more in ecclesiastical matters, despite the protestations of the pope. Jansenism made fresh advances and established an independent Church in Holland. Limited now to spiritual weapons, Rome found it very difficult to fight against the "enlightened" despots of Europe and the attacks became all the fiercer in proportion to the stronger reaction of the Church. Clement XIII cannot be too greatly admired for the constancy with which he underlined the dangers of a science and a philosophy which were becoming more and more detached from the supernatural. He condemned the *De l'Esprit* of Helvétius, and Rousseau's *Émile*, and denounced the peril which the works of the Encyclopedists presented. The establishment of public veneration of the Sacred Heart in 1765 was, under those conditions, not only the definite sanction of a form of piety which had been generally practised for nearly one hundred years, but also a timely initiative against rationalism and a withering Jansenism. So it was at the very moment when the Jesuits were sinking under the weight of the attacks upon them, that official recognition was given to a devotion which they had done much to spread.

It was not surprising that on the death of Clement XIII, the conclave was subjected to manoeuvres intended to ensure the election of a pope hostile to the Jesuits. The next pope, who insisted on taking the name of Clement XIV, had agreed, it would seem, that their suppression could be envisaged with a clear conscience. His tactics were to make some concessions to the Catholic governments in order to have them as allies in the struggle against dechristianization. It could be seen, however, where the pope's sympathies really lay from his Brief of July 12th, 1769, encouraging the missionary work of the Society in heathen countries. This was too much for the French and Spanish governments. The sovereigns themselves insisted in threatening tones on the abolition of the Jesuits. Clement XIV, taking as a pretext certain aspects of Jesuit activities open to criticism, adopted a series of measures against them with a view to gaining time. But a threat of schism and a veritable summons from the Spanish Court to take action, put an end to the pope's resistance. On July 21st, 1773, the Brief *Dominus ac Redemptor*, suppressed the Society of Jesus, and some of their leaders were even arrested. A Jesuit Father acknowledged that in Clement XIV's position, he would have done the same: his Order had been sacrificed to save the Church from a greater evil.

A paradoxical situation arose when the King of Prussia, Frederick II, and the Czarina, Catherine II, forbade the bishops to publish the Brief in parts of their dominions and thus made it possible for the Jesuits to continue to exist.

Despite Clement XIV's hopes, his surrender, far from bringing him help against agnosticism and the tendency to schism, was interpreted as a prelude to further concessions.

He died saddened by the growth of hatred, by the partition of Poland, in which he saw with sorrow the cooperation of Austria, by the spread of Jansenism in the latter country, above all by the futility, in a word, of willing sacrifice.

His successor, Pius VI (1775–99), took up a heavy burden and was destined to know more painful anguish and a still more bitter end, since he died in exile after ten years of revolutions, which are not to be dealt with in this book. In the period with which we are concerned, his principal anxieties were the ever rising tide of Deism and unbelief, Febronianism, Josephism, and the hostile attitude of Tuscany and Naples. Febronius (who will be described in the following chapter), whose theories came close to Gallicanism, had seen his book put on the Index of 1764. He had then recanted, but his ideas had spread, cropping up again in the archbishops of Cologne, Trier and Mainz. When the Duke of Bavaria established a nunciature at Munich, to avoid some of his subjects coming under the jurisdiction of foreign bishops, these three prelates, joined by the archbishop of Salzburg, reacted against a possible interference of the nuncio in their jurisdictions. They united their efforts to establish a code of rules to govern the relations between the German Church and Rome. The Emperor Joseph II supported their action, and this became the subject of a congress held at Ems. From this congress there issued a report hostile to the nuncios and recommending reforms in many directions. The struggle with Rome had still not been settled when the French invaded the Rhine dioceses in 1792.

What was called Josephism was actually the application of Febronian ideas by the Emperor, and it will be seen later how these were developed. Maria Theresa had already shown this tendency, but her son, Joseph II, went very much further, well beyond what even the most extreme supporters of Gallicanism had ever thought of achieving in France. Combining

genuine faith with admiration for the most unbelieving philosophers, his was a strange mind in which there coexisted, but
never harmonized, absolutist traditions and a desire to move
with his times. He was, indeed, one of those men who considered that the pope was a personage whose feet should be
kissed but whose hands should be tied. It was not enough for
him to escape from the authority of Rome; he wished to
govern his Church himself. In order to arrive at a reasonable
solution Pius VI agreed to come to Vienna, a most extraordinary step on his part, but it was in vain. However, the
subjects of Joseph II themselves were beginning to show their
disapproval by the time his brother Leopold II, Duke of
Tuscany, succeeded him. While Duke of Tuscany Leopold
had introduced into his duchy not a few of the principles of
Josephism, yet strangely enough, despite his general agreement with his brother Joseph's policy, to all intents and purposes he reversed it on becoming Emperor. Yet not
completely, as some trace of Josephism remained until very
late into the nineteenth century.

Curiously enough, the accession of Leopold to the imperial
throne, in 1790, put an end to a similar crisis which he had
provoked in his Tuscan duchy. The clergy there certainly laid
themselves open to criticism, but Leopold wished to deal
with this matter himself, being supported in his views by
Scipio de Ricci, the Jansenist and Gallican bishop of Pistoia.
The Synod, which was held in that town in 1786, adopted a
series of reforms, some of which were inspired by the four
articles of 1682, while the others were definitely Jansenist.
These reforms were rejected by a National Synod at Florence
in 1787, to the great resentment of Leopold, and they were
probably on the point of being enforced by him when he
became emperor and the movement collapsed, though not
without leaving traces of the Jansenist spirit in the Italian
clergy.

And so the Church, just at the moment when great disasters were near at hand, saw its authority contested by the very persons who should have been its most loyal supporters, and who, through attempting to run with the wind, found themselves swept away by it.

CHAPTER XIV

OLD DISPUTES AND THE

NEW SPIRIT

It is a strange thing that the most serious obstacles encountered by the Church during the eighteenth century were just the same as those that it had found in its path in the preceding century. But the comparison between them is like that of diseases of which the virulence has increased while the whole body has become weaker, and when the help on which it should have normally been able to rely was found lacking. That is why it is still necessary to study former manifestations such as Jansenism and Gallicanism in their development and their later phases, together with what has been called the new spirit, although all that was new about it was its popularity.

The Jansenist controversy, which had died down after the "Clementine Peace", revived at the beginning of the eighteenth century. During the year 1701, a "case of conscience" had been submitted to the Doctors of the Sorbonne, namely: could absolution be given to a penitent who considered that the five condemned propositions did not appear in the book by Jansenius, and who, keeping a respectful silence on this point, had signed the formulary of Alexander VII with that mental reservation. Forty Doctors replied in the affirmative but their opinion, when printed, provoked a lively reaction from a number of bishops, including Bossuet and Fénelon, and the condemnation by Clement XI of "the case of conscience".

As this matter grew more serious, Louis XIV obtained from the pope the Bull *Vineam Domini*, declaring that respectful silence was not enough, and demanding a denial "by word and conscience" of the five propositions, which were held to be part of the doctrine of Jansenius. The Clergy Assembly accepted the Bull but with reservations which called into question the authority of pontifical decisions, so long as the bishops had not accepted them. The pope vainly protested against this attitude, but the main thing was that the Bull, for the moment at any rate, was obeyed. The nuns of Port-Royal, who no longer recruited further subjects but had constituted themselves the vigilant and anxious guardians of treasured traditions, refused to sign a formula of acceptance unless it contained the words "without prejudice to the peace of Clement IX". This opposition infuriated the king, who obtained an interdict on the convent in 1707, and then had the nuns driven out (1709), their buildings totally destroyed and even their cemetery laid waste. The brutality and the action taken against these aged and pious women, who lived quite apart from the world without any defence, created great scandal and helped the Jansenist cause rather than otherwise.

This was seen when a fresh matter, no longer of merely local interest, arose to swell the dispute. The Oratorian Quesnel (1634–1719) in 1671 had published a learned commentary on the Gospels, which was revised and expanded several times until it was finally printed as a book, in 1693, under the title of *Réflexions morales sur le Nouveau Testament*. Clever writing concealed the harmfulness of the text, and the author had also been skilful enough to combine with it theories approximating to those of Richerism on the government of the Church, calculated to obtain for him the support of the Gallicans. The book proved a great success, particularly as it gained the approval of Louis-Antoine de Noailles, bishop of

Châlons. But in 1708 it was censured by Clement XI, and Noailles, who meanwhile had been made a cardinal and archbishop of Paris, was instructed to withdraw his approval. In view of his hesitation in doing so, Louis XIV requested Rome to examine the book again, with the result that it was formally condemned in the Bull *Unigenitus* of September 8th, 1713, rejecting 101 propositions taken from *Réflexions morales*. Outside France the matter was considered settled, but Noailles, while revoking his approval, maintained that certain propositions of Quesnel, considered individually, could be regarded as orthodox. He, along with other bishops, refused to accept the Bull until further clarifications had been obtained. The dispute grew to such proportions that Fénelon advised the king to appeal to the pope for a meeting of the National Council, but the death of Louis XIV, in 1715, brought this project to naught. The Regent (1715–23), a sceptical and frivolous prince, allowed the opposition to grow. In 1717, four Gallican bishops called for a General Council, and they were supported by the Universities of Paris, Nantes and Rheims, and by a very large number of ecclesiastics and laymen. Cardinal Noailles himself appealed "from" the pope who was manifestly mistaken and from the Bull *Unigenitus* "to" the better-informed pope and a free General Council. France was thus divided into "acceptors" and "appealers" (*appelants*) and there was a real danger of a schism. Clement XI, in his Bull *Pastoralis officii*, excommunicated the *appelants*, but the latter appealed again against the later Bull and contested the validity of the excommunication. The position was so serious that the regent, on the advice of Cardinal Dubois, stopped the development of a situation which he had allowed to take place, and caused the Bull *Unigenitus* to receive its *exsequatur* so that it might have the force of law (1720). Noailles only submitted fully as late as 1728, and some recalcitrants still remained, sustained in their beliefs by miraculous ecstasies and healings which were said to have taken place on the tomb of the Jansenist deacon Pâris, who had died in 1727 (these were the convulsionaries of the cemetery of Saint-Médard).

With the new administration of Cardinal Fleury, there was cooperation between Church and State to suppress Jansenism, but it had left lasting traces even on those who did not openly profess it. It cannot be said that its spirit is quite extinct even now, as it is possible to trace back to it a narrow conception of religion and requirements prejudicial to frequentation of the sacraments. At the time itself, there was still persistent hostility to the Jesuits and even to Rome.

Jansenism, in any case, had moments of revival and continued for a very long time. Its faithful had their journal and their secret funds (their Perrette money-box, named after Nicole's housekeeper), and they found numerous supporters in the parliamentary world.

In this way can be explained the violent flare-up in the middle of the century over the question of confession certificates, which originated in the refusal by several priests to give the sacraments to the dying who refused to accept the Bull *Unigenitus*, or who could not produce, on this matter, a certificate from a duly qualified confessor. The opponents of this practice, instead of appealing to the religious authorities, applied to Parliament, which had the audacity to support them and began an extremely violent campaign against the archbishop of Paris, Christopher de Beaumont. After a conflict lasting many years, during which the king, owing to lack of authority, gave his support now to the archbishop and now to Parliament, Benedict XIV tried to achieve a settlement by declaring that, while obedience to the Bull *Unigenitus* remained obligatory, there was no reason to refuse the sacraments except in the case of such opposers as had caused scandal by their notorious attitude. Shortly afterwards, the king held a "bed of justice" which gave the force of law to the pope's decision, and the quarrel subsided only to begin again for the last time in 1767, when it ended in the exile of the Parliamentarians (1771). Although the episcopate had won, this dispute, which had grown more political than religious, had the very serious result of bringing Parliament into opposition with the monarchy.

If Jansenism had caused most stir and trouble in France, at least it subsided without causing schism. The same cannot be said for Holland. The intellectual climate there was favourable to the formation of sects, and Jansenism benefited from the hostility shown by the Dutch clergy to the Jesuits, who had come from other countries as missionaries. It is significant that men like Arnauld and Quesnel should have taken refuge in Holland. The vicar apostolic of Utrecht, who was a Jansenist, entrusted to Arnauld the work of training a number of clerics of distinction, amongst them one Peter Codde, who succeeded him as vicar apostolic. The new vicar was so suspect that Clement XI deposed him in 1702. A pro-vicar nominated by Rome was attacked so fiercely by the States General and by the clergy, that he had to leave the country in 1704. After the death of Codde in 1710, the vicariate council of Utrecht, which had been reconstituted into a metropolitan chapter, was in charge of a Church already practically separated from Rome, and the schism was completed in 1723 by the election of Cornelius Steenoven, the vicar-general, as archbishop of Utrecht. Steenoven received episcopal consecration from a Jansenist bishop, Varlet, who had previously been suspended from office. One of Steenoven's successors created two suffragan bishoprics at Haarlem and at Deventer. This Church is still in existence and its faithful, who number several thousands, describe themselves as "Old Roman Catholics".

Jansenism also penetrated into Italy, and even to Rome, which is surprising when it is remembered how constant was the policy of Rome in this respect. This was because Rome, where many missions converge and where many cases are pleaded, was the precise spot where the advocates of Jansenism could meet together. Even among the very entourage of the pope, especially that of Benedict XIV, the holders of this doctrine had their discreet, but useful, protectors. However it would seem that the sympathy shown by them was not on the doctrinal level, but was aroused more by admiration for the lofty moral requirements demands of Jansenism. It is permissible to think that, in this field, Jansenism was able to contribute to the preservation of certain values in Italy. On the other hand, there is no doubt that these tendencies created an atmosphere inimical to the Jesuits and prepared the ground for the abolition of the Society of Jesus.

The history of the Jansenist quarrel is a good illustration of how a doctrinal question can assume a definite political nature and so become one of the major preoccupations of the temporal power. In France particularly, we have seen that this power did not always support the views of Rome, and that these encroachments led to a fear that a national Church might be set up. In the first half of the eighteenth century, all the Bourbon monarchies showed this tendency, as indeed did all the Latin courts. Thus, in Spain, by the Concordats of 1737 and 1743, the State encroached on ecclesiastical jurisdiction and made of the Inquisition a kind of state organism. This occurred also in Portugal, where the Government laid its hands on Church properties, and likewise in the Italian courts.

As in the previous century, this policy had its theoreticians. In 1707, there appeared the *Traité de la Puissance Ecclésiastique et Temporelle* of the French author, Ellies du Pin; in 1714, the *Du Témoignage de la Vérité dans l'Église*, of the Oratorian, Vivien de la Borde; in 1753, the *Jus ecclesiasticum universum*, the massive work of the Flemish canonist Z. B. Van Espen. In this latter work, the divine right of kings is praised to the detriment of papal authority, which is regarded as a purely human creation. Naturally, the monarchy did nothing to hinder the distribution of these works.

What is new towards the middle of the century is that this tendency also gained ground in Germany, where the theories just mentioned were taken up in a work published in Frankfurt in 1763, entitled *De statu ecclesiae et legitima potestate Romani Pontificis.* The author, who had concealed himself under the pseudonym of Justinus Febronius, was Johann Nikolaus von Hontheim, coadjutor of the Prince-Bishop Elector of Trier. Adapting the Gallican doctrine to existing conditions in Germany, he put forward the opinion that unity of faith would only be restored when the Church found again the organization that it possessed in the earliest days of Christianity. The government of the Church belonged to the bishops assembled in the Council, and the pope, who was not infallible, had only honorary primacy. Consequently, decisions of the latter were only of value when they were supported by the open or tacit adhesion of the whole Church and were binding only on such national churches and dioceses as had accepted them. Recognition was given to the rights of the popes in regard to the protection of faith and unity, but everything connected with church administration should revert to the bishops, and be regained by them, with the help of the Catholic princes if need be.

This book caused a great sensation. By depicting the institutions of the Church as very fluid in its earliest days, with their present condition the result of a series of usurpations, it raised the possibility of adaptations in such a way as to appeal to those who were anxious to move with the times. It also gave satisfaction to old German rancours regarding Roman authority and financial matters, and it was not by accident that it emanated from the entourage of a prince-bishop.

In imagining that his theories would be able to restore the unity of the Church, Hontheim was very much mistaken, since they left untouched the dogmatic issues. This was so obviously true that he was vigorously opposed by the Protestants themselves. But, in the Catholic world, governments were so anxious for his book to succeed that they smoothed its path for him, even to the extent of having it translated and distributed in the Bourbon countries and elsewhere.

Naturally, Rome condemned it again and again. In the Latin Countries, Febronianism did little more than consolidate the Gallican position, already under heavy attack, but, in Germany, it gave force to the developments which the sovereigns had already begun, and led to the ridiculous excesses of Josephism.

It is well known what a great struggle Maria-Theresa had, even in making certain of the crown, guaranteed to her by many treaties, and what difficult problems she had to face owing to the heterogeneous character of her States. It is quite natural that, under these conditions, she should have wished to coordinate her reforms. Deeply religious by nature, she wished very sincerely to justify the title of "Apostolic Majesty", with which Clement XIII had honoured her in 1758. Among her aims were the provision of guarantees for Church property and the religious life, and the improvement of the training of the clergy. But, already influenced by Jansenist ideas, she had the misfortune to be surrounded by disciples of Febronius or by men won over by the new philosophy. Among the former must be mentioned the Benedictine Abbot of Braunau, Rautenstrauch, and among the latter, her doctor, the Dutchman Van Swieten, a Jansenist and very hostile to the Jesuits. At their instigation, the goods of the Church were administered by the State, and the clergy increasingly became mere civil servants. On governmental initiative, the number of religious houses, excessive in any case, was reduced; it was forbidden to take vows before the age of twenty-four; the clergy were made to pay taxes; and the publication of pontifical decrees was forbidden without prior authorization by the civil authorities. But these reforms are not wholly to be criticized, as Rautenstrauch did much to develop among the clergy the study, until then neglected, of patristics and pastoral theology. But, by putting the seminaries under State control and by proscribing scholasticism, which he did not like, he created the atmosphere in which Josephism was able to develop.

The good intentions of Joseph II, a pious, even a devout, prince, can be no more doubted than were those of his mother. But, under his tutors with rationalist leanings, and later surrounded by Freemasons and Illuminati, this admirer of Frederick II made of religion the major object of his unenlightened despotism. There is some ingenuity in the pretensions of this narrow-minded man, who pruned the Master's vine to his fashion and to the current taste. Fully convinced that he must give to God the things which are God's and to Caesar the things which are Caesar's, he was also convinced that God, in his infinite wisdom, had entrusted to Caesar the mission of carrying this out. When dealing with this matter, he was guided by the philosophers whose ideas supported this wise ordinance. And since there is no proper order without authority, he wished, assured of his lights, to govern a Church indeed, but one which must be his Church. Thus, in the case of Joseph II, Febronius had been left well behind. The latter, in direct proportion to the extent by which he undermined pontifical authority, allotted an eminent rôle to the episcopate, especially in matters of dogma and discipline, and, in his proposal for a return to the primitive Church, he dreamt of a renewal of spirituality in a freed and active Christianity.

The emperor, on the other hand, wished to make his bishops into obedient functionaries, as has already been seen, but also—and this it is which is new, and reveals his true nature—to control the whole ecclesiastical administration even down to the smallest ceremonial details. "My brother, the sacristan", Frederick said of this emperor, who insisted on episcopal instructions being submitted to him, who controlled processions, the number of Masses to be said in churches and chapels, and the number of candles to be lit for specific services. It is possible to smile at these petty details if that religious policy, of which these were such minor items, had not tended to detach the Church from some of its traditions and to introduce into it some of the new philosophy. For this is just what Joseph II, the unwitting puppet of his entourage, achieved, by identifying mysticism with fanaticism, contemplation with laziness, and by ordering the closing of more than 600 religious houses; by forbidding pilgrimages; by selling blessed relics and vessels; by instituting civil marriage and allowing divorce. The idea of abolishing everything which might appear to be useless luxury and superstition, by using the goods of the suppressed monasteries for charitable purposes, and also by granting to Protestants and to the Orthodox in his States their civil rights and liberty to conduct their own worship in private, all these actions tended to make the Church tolerable to the philosophers. Must it be said with Voltaire after all this, that, by these deeds the German Holy Roman Empire was no longer either Holy or Roman? This facile jest greatly exaggerates the truth. Certain of Joseph II's reforms were good ones; reorganization of the seminaries, creation of numerous parishes in neglected districts, these, for example, had lasting consequences. But it was unfortunate, on the eve of great upheavals, that the authority of the Holy See should be so flouted and that the unity of the Church should show such visible cracks. Towards the end of his reign, the subjects of Joseph II began to be aware of this. In the Austrian Lowlands, very hostile to his innovations, there was an uprising, and Joseph II died (1790) at the moment when, in the empire, the episcopate began to react with vigour.

Doctrinal disputes and government interference were certainly harmful to the Church, but they attested to the importance given to Christian values and to dogmas by their very variety, ranging in subject from error to excessive zeal. It was quite a different matter with Deism and rationalism, which were such clearly marked characteristics of eighteenth-century thought. Pascal had already expressed this same idea when he said of Deism that "it was as much removed from the Christian religion as was atheism, which is in direct opposition to it". It has already been seen how, in the previous century, the new scientific and philosophical advances had sown doubts in intellectual circles about revealed truth, and had given birth to a critical spirit, to a sense of the relative, which led directly to indifference. At the same time, escaping from the tutelage of religion, intellectual life, institutions and society developed in their individual fashion taking reason as their guide and for their laws those of nature. This tendency, particularly strong in England after the seventeenth century, quickly spread to France and to Germany. It would be pure sectarianism to deny the good effects it had. The ideal of truth and humanity held by the philosophers made a large contribution towards the disappearance of many superstitions, notably sorcery, towards the suppression of torture, and towards the spread of toleration. Religion itself has profited from it, through the elimination of quasi-fetishistic practices and of excessive belief in miracles. But it suffered far more than it benefited.

It would be outside the scope of this book to study the paths which these new ideas have followed, but it is useful to recall their main features. The Englishman, Francis Bacon (1561–1626), made a distinction between the field of faith and that of reason, and eliminated the divine element from the study of nature and the search for happiness, all of which contributed to the secularization of philosophical thinking. Descartes (1596–1650), although a devout Christian, took as his starting point systematic doubt, and so developed the critical spirit that he became the source of a whole rationalist stream which penetrated even into ecclesiastical circles. In the case of both these men, the search for truth took no account of revelation. From that time onwards, those who sought for God by the sole light of reason, arrived at a point called Deism, a natural religion which is first set forth in coherent terms in the works of Herbert of Cherbury (1582–1648), notably in his *De Veritate*. A God exists, who of necessity punishes evil and whom one must serve by doing good. Anything additional to these ideas has come from man's imagination. In Holland, the Jew, Spinoza (1632–77), said just the same thing about the Bible, and, with him, religion became a kind of natural pantheism, arousing in man feelings of love and respect. The influence of Spinoza was strong in the eighteenth century especially among German intellectuals.

But it is mainly to England that one returns in the search for new and active centres of this philosophy. This was no accidental development. After the disturbances of the Civil War and the Commonwealth, the Restoration had been a time of dissolute, libertinous living, and the Revolution of 1688, by enlarging freedom of conscience, and shortly afterwards, freedom of the press, had made that country the most suitable place for independent thinking, including what is now called free thinking. It should be noted, incidentally, that there is a shade of difference in the meaning now given to the term freethinker and that originally given to it, when it simply meant total lack of submission to the Established Church. Even before the Revolution of 1688, Thomas Hobbes (1588–1679) had preached a materialism in which there was no longer any place for religion, which he looked on as being merely a means for keeping the people in subjection. If an exception be made of Locke (1632–1704), still in favour of Christianity (*The Reasonableness of Christianity*, 1695), the English philosophers of this period, notably John Toland (1670–1722) and Matthew Tyndall (1657–1733), were definitely Deists.

However, towards the middle of the century, under the influence of Methodism, which will be mentioned later, many English people returned to revelation, while scepticism grew stronger among others, a development to which David Hume (1711–76) greatly contributed.

It is not surprising that it was in Great Britain, where freedom of assembly encouraged meetings in coffee houses and clubs, that freemasonry found, if not its origin, at any rate its modern form. Without going back as far as the builders of Solomon's Temple, it did indeed take its inspiration from the traditions of the lodges of cathedral builders. If the groups which were thus set up in Scotland and in England at the beginning of the eighteenth century were primarily intellectual, it would appear that the original lodges may have worked to support the cause of the Stuarts, which may have accounted for their secrecy, whereas the Grand Lodge of England supported the Hanoverian policy. Sister lodges set up on the Continent, in France and Italy where the Stuarts were living, continued this political activity. This is probably the reason for the anti-Catholic attitude of some of the British lodges. Otherwise the ideal of the brotherhood of man held by the freemasons, showed itself generally in a vague form of Deism. Consequently, helped by the influence of local variations, it can be understood why many Catholics, even priests, were able to be masons without scruples of conscience. This was all the more so, since, in addition to its philanthropic intentions, which it would be unjust to deny, there must be added the attraction of a seductive secrecy and also of a philosophy which seemed to be a mark of progress. But in Catholic countries, the lodges soon became hostile towards the Church and, although invoking the Great Architect of the Universe, towards religion, and finally became centres of rationalism, to such an extent that Clement XII, in 1738 in his Bull *In Eminenti*, forbade the faithful to belong to these secret societies, under pain of excommunication. This prohibition was renewed on many subsequent occasions. In fact everything happened as if these associations, whose principle was by no means anti-religious, had chosen to assume a position which, owing to contemporary tendencies, both political and intellectual, was difficult to change. In a different climate of opinion, which the Church may help to bring about, is it rash to think of freemasonry which, going back to its original tenets, may become one more Christian fraternity?

However definite may have been the influence of English thinking in France, it was only one of the factors, and by no means the biggest, in the evolution of thought. On the contrary, it would have been surprising if the faith had remained untouched, especially among the privileged classes and in intellectual circles. It is not paradoxical in this context to incriminate the discouraging severity of Jansenism in equal measure with the frivolity of the Court. In view of the number of clerics who were dazzled by the new philosophy, one can only quote Juvenal's *quis custodiat ipsos custodes?*

It must be recognized that this new philosophy was supported by men of wisdom and talent, to whom, in general, were opposed men of mediocre polemic ability, poorly equipped, as theology itself was then very much in decline. At the very end of the seventeenth century there had appeared the *Dictionnaire historique et critique* of the Huguenot, Peter Bayle (1647–1706), which was very widely read. Its attacks on religion were all the more devastating because their wide dispersion throughout the book made them seem less systematic. Montesquieu (1689–1755), in his *Lettres persanes* (1721), in an exotic Eastern setting, mocked political institutions as well as the Church, but, in his later works, he showed himself very appreciative of the social usefulness of religious principles. His irony was certainly bitter, but it gives no impression of hatred. The same cannot be said of Voltaire (1694–1778), whose many-sided talent and incomparable zest were systematically employed, during his long life, against

the Church and against Christianity in general. The eighteenth
century has been called the century of Voltaire, which gives
an idea of his intellectual supremacy, and so of his influence.
The word "voltairian" was then coined, and it is significant
that there is no ambiguity about the accepted anti-religious
meaning of that word. After his stay in England, however,
Voltaire returned a Deist.

On the other hand, it is atheism and systematic hostility,
however skilfully dispersed, which makes of the twenty-eight
volumes and seven supplements of the *Encyclopédie* (1751–
80), a magnificent work nevertheless, such a formidable
engine of war against religion in general, and Catholicism in
particular. Diderot (1713–84) and D'Alembert (1717–83), who
were the great undertakers of this publication, professed the
most absolute irreligion. So did also, Condillac, La Mettrie,
friend of Frederick II and author of *Homme machine* (1748),
Helvétius, *De l'esprit* (1778), and especially Baron d'Holbach,
of whom it has been said that his *Système de la nature* (1770)
is the atheist's Bible.

By comparison with these materialist philosophers, whose
barren nature makes them incapable of understanding that religion can be a necessity and that this need is already one
reason for believing, Jean-Jacques Rousseau (1712–78) at-
tracts by his sensitiveness and his anxious mind. But his
very attractiveness was also his danger. Born in a Huguenot
family in Geneva, he was for some time a Catholic, but only
very superficially. For him, man was not only a being of
reason but also of feeling. In fact, his religion was the love
of the beautiful and the good. He believed in the existence
of God and in the immortality of the soul, but also in the
fundamental goodness of man. His was the religion of nature,
and, in that respect, he was a child of the century of light. If
his religious philosophy had so many admirers, this was because it was accompanied by a burning faith in democracy
at a moment when nations were seeking for a new social

order. To that extent, with the other philosophers mentioned above, he was one of the promoters of the French Revolution.

Many reasons contributed to the speedy and wide diffusion of these new doctrines—the comparative leniency of the government, the influence of the salons, the thirst for reading, and the wish to escape from authority, whether temporal or otherwise. Emphasis must be laid on this frame of mind; a strange mixture of snobbery, calculation and naïvety, which consisted in a readiness to lay down one's arms to the enemy, and with compromise after compromise, surrender the position to him. Snobbery, to use a word which did not then exist, seemed to be an aspiration to move with one's times or even to seek to be in the forefront: calculation, that was to believe it was good tactics to welcome new ideas so as to be their master, but naïvety, because one soon became their prisoner. It was in this spirit that Abbé de Bernis corresponded in a friendly manner with Voltaire, while the aristocracy flocked to see themselves ridiculed in the *Mariage de Figaro*. But, in every age, what a large number of people have eyes with which they do not see, and, even today, is this not the error of a certain kind of progress?

The welcome given to the philosophers by Frederick II, the philosopher king, is well known, and that too, given by Joseph II, although he was a Catholic. It is true that Germany had not waited for inspiration from abroad before attacking revealed religion. Christian Wolff (1679–1754), a second-rate popularizer of Leibniz, despised by Frederick William I but protected by Frederick II, was teaching, with deplorable success, at the University of Halle, that reason must be the only guide in matters of religion. Lorenz Schmidt, when publishing a translation of the Bible called the Wertheim Bible (1725), gave a rationalist commentary on it, and following his opinions, Protestant theologians denied all supernatural character to the holy Scriptures.

This was the beginning of a whole series of rationalist exegetists from the German Universities. Among the general public, what the Encyclopedia had done in France was finally accomplished by Christopher Nicolai and his *Deutsche Allgemeine Bibliothek*. Lessing and Kant, born into this atmosphere, completed its work by giving it the hall-marks of their genius. It must not be imagined that Catholic circles escaped free. Not only in Germany and Bohemia, but even in the Iberian Peninsula and in Italy, those very men whose mission it was to train the clergy, were often impregnated with rationalist philosophy. If Brunetière was able to write that the eighteenth century was the least Christian in the history of France, the same remark can be truthfully applied to the whole of Europe.

CHAPTER XV

THE ARK IN THE STORM

It appears, therefore, as if the Church experienced greater dangers in the eighteenth century than at the time of the Reformation, when they were more localized. Rationalist ideas, with a tendency towards disbelief and indifference, were universally held, while the encroachment of governments on ecclesiastical matters was most marked in the Catholic countries themselves. On the other hand, the papacy was no longer giving such distressing personal examples as had done much harm to its prestige in the opening years of modern times, and the clergy as a whole, being better instructed, showed in their lives devotion and virtue. The exceptions, mainly among the higher clergy, must not allow it to be forgotten that this century also saw a blossoming of sanctity.

In Italy, the faith had retained a popular character, being, that is to say, very exteriorized. The clergy, great in number, included many religious without a true vocation, and priests without a charge, whose manner of life was not always exemplary. But the century was marked by a number of apostles whom the Church has raised to its altars, worthy successors to Gregory Barbarigo (1625–97), the heroic bishop of Padua: the Jesuit, Francis Geronimo (1643–1716), who preached with convincing fervour mainly at Naples, the Franciscan, Leonard of Port-Maurice (1676–1751), Paul of the Cross (1694–1775), founder of the Passionists, and, especially, Alphonsus

Liguori (1696–1787), founder of the Redemptorists and author of a treatise on moral theology, a work which, frequently revised, followed a middle course, full of wisdom, between Jansenist severity and laxism. A disciple of his in Austria, Clement Mary Hofbauer (1751–1821), fought nobly against Josephism and rationalism.

In Spain, where also the clergy were numerous, and often ignorant and irresponsible, introducing into their preaching and ministry familiarities in bad taste, the faith was boisterously extrovert but it was also childish and full of superstition. Enlightened ministers such as Aranda and Florida Blanca put obstacles in the way of the initiative of the bishops by their encroaching State control.

The picture of France in this period, with its people of a different nature, its greater stage of development, and its openness to every influence, presents a notable contrast to Italy and Spain. There is also a striking difference over the years, since, up to the middle sixties of the century, religious interest was still strong enough for the country to be disturbed by questions of dogma, as has been seen in the Jansenist problem. Later on, Christians themselves, whether they were interested simply in the scientific and philosophical movement, or concerned about the problems which that movement presented to their faith, were much less preoccupied about what they regarded as theological subtleties at a time when their belief in God was already shaken. In their anxiety to find a scientific and sociological justification for it, they gave the impression of being more alive, henceforward, to the practical side of religion. Hence the importance of the works of Abbé Bergier (*Examen du matérialisme*) and of Le Gros (*Examen des ouvrages de J. J. Rousseau*), showing that the progress of the human spirit in general, as well as that of the individual, excludes a more perfect original state. From this also, comes the stress placed on the need for a reasoned faith, and on the happiness which would be found by society from a strict observance of evangelical teachings. Certain apologists strike a very modern note, such as, for instance, Abbé Terrasson who, taking up the theme of Fontenelle on the plurality of worlds, visualizes planets on one of which the inhabitants are in the same state as man was before the Fall; or on another planet, after man had sinned; and, on another one still, after the Redemption.

But there was another contrast in France in the eighteenth century, which could hardly be suspected from reading history books, and that was between the ideas and customs which have attracted so much attention and have been put forward as typical, and the well-established traditions which were probably followed by the majority of the people. The encroachment of the temporal power into religious matters had not prevented the clergy from remaining a strong social power, both on account of their solid organization and by reason of the great amount of property they held, some fifth of the whole country, with immense revenues arising therefrom. These riches were not without their dangers, as could be seen in many monasteries, in which the commendatory abbot waxed fat without being in residence, and where the religious ideal no longer existed. It was not this wealth which really mattered, however, but the faith which had remained firmly anchored in so many French hearts. The eighteenth century in France has been very much maligned, because it has been badly known. Great insistence has been given to its philosophers, to the dominance of Voltaire and the influence of Rousseau; while it has been the worse sides of the character of Louis XV, and the frivolity of an age of ribbons and powder which have been emphasized. This is rather like asserting that jazz, strip-tease, scandalous novels and worthless paintings would be the only things to survive from our present century. On the contrary, for anyone who studies it carefully, ignoring pithy anecdotes, in an effort to reconstitute the everyday life of that period, France would then appear as a country of hard and wholesome work, with great administrators inspired with ideals for the common good; with honest artists; with artisans anxious to produce good work, and where family life revealed itself as based on simple but solid virtues. The sugary sentimentality of a man like Greuze probably contributed to the spread of the idea that his paintings were social comedies, with their pretence of conventional treatment. Actually, he succeeded in getting the gamblers and cynics to take a rest for awhile from their fooleries, and the fact that he was so popular calls for some reflection. In any case, is there not a good touchstone to see how deep and how widely spread religious feeling then was? This is to be found in the persecution of the revolutionary period, which was surely the real moment of truth. There is a whole range of irrefutable witness of secret religious steadfastness to the point of combat and even martyrdom. These realities are well known, because historical research always pays greater attention to periods of great upheaval. But the conclusion is obvious. Matters would have been very different throughout that century had not belief in God—for even the Revolution admitted the existence of a Supreme Being—and also loyalty to the Church been much more widespread than is sometimes alleged nowadays. Even though this has been made clear, it is still regrettable that far too little work has been done on the history of the French Church and on the religious life of France in the eighteenth century. It is true that the Revolution itself and its consequences caused the disappearance of many documents, but research work, so far as it has gone up to the present, has given encouraging results, and there is a reasonable possibility of a religious map of France at the end of the *ancien régime,* being one day drawn.

The traditional faith thus persisted, upheld by certain great bishops, such as Christopher de Beaumont, archbishop of Paris, and Louis de la Motte, bishop of Amiens. It can still be thought that it was an unfortunate development which witnessed the complete exclusion of the poorer classes from the episcopate, whereas, in the seventeenth century, some of the most renowned prelates had not come from the nobility. The faith was maintained by clergy and by laymen who felt it their duty to show ever more devotion as impiety increased. On the eve of the Revolution there was even a new upsurge of the faith, probably due to the influence of the mystics, which was as far removed as it could be from Jansenism, as will be described later. It is to be hoped that an historian will be found who will carry on the work of Abbé Bremond to a later period. As far as can be seen, there might emerge from this work a picture of a Christian France, so far hardly suspected, but of which there are already indications in the multiplication of religious brotherhoods, of secular institutes, of Marian devotions and of the growing cultus of the Sacred Heart.

But when the life of the clergy is studied in that period, what great contrasts there are, especially among the priests in the towns. Even without making reference to the scandalous priests, important and unimportant, who are only too well known, it suffices to call to mind the three hundred ecclesiastics attached to the parish of Saint-Sulpice for ludicrous duties, and to set against them the figure of Jacques-André Emery, at the seminary of the same name. Monsieur Emery (1732–1811), that splendid character, was, in the first place, one of the few people who opposed the brilliant writing of the Encyclopedists with something more than third-rate apologetics or sickly moral stories, with extracts chosen from the works of other great, but temporarily forgotten, Christian philosophers. When he was elected Superior-General of Saint-Sulpice in 1782, he found the seminary mainly engaged in worldly vanities, and set about imposing a strict rule, not without encountering lively opposition. He contributed to the mystical revival by publishing, still in the form of extracts, his book called *L'Esprit de Sainte Thérèse*. But he was chiefly noted for the great influence he had on those around him and, fortunately, the activity of this very great animator continued during the Revolution and under the Empire.

Perhaps very little will ever be known about the country clergy, so important in a country which had remained largely agricultural, since their humble existence has left very few written records. Their influence had been increased by the extension of their duties, since the parish priest had been put in control of the civil registers and it was through him, in most cases, that administrative regulations were transmitted. The village priest at the beginning of the seventeenth century, generally poor and uninstructed, was, in the eighteenth century, thanks to the seminaries, better educated than most of his parishioners, on whom he exercised a great moral influence. Inventories of the years before the Revolution reveal that the works of the philosophers had penetrated into many presbyteries, and not only those of the town clergy. Furthermore, it is found, particularly in the second half of the century, that the country parish priest was no longer isolated. He was aware of his importance to the nation and, in cooperation with his colleagues, he intended to have his rights, until then largely neglected by the episcopate, acknowledged. In this he could rely on the help of the important work and the consultations of the lay canonist, Maultrot. In any case Maultrot was a follower of Richer, holding that it was from God himself, and not from the bishops, that parish priests held authority over their parishioners. The parish priests could also rely on the syndical organizations, which were actually illicit, for the defence of their material interests. In this respect, in spite of the increase in the "adequate emolument", there still persisted some bitterness on the part of the priest-in-charge against the "great-tithe" owner. In too many villages, the priest lived sparsely, hardly any better than, and sometimes not nearly as well as the peasants. Sharing in this way the same worries, pastor and faithful were at one in their demands, and it was the priests in many cases who inspired the latter in drawing up their list of grievances. With this state of mind at one end of the scale and many prelates of easy virtue or influenced by the new philosophy at the other, it can be imagined that the representatives of the clergy, obviously chosen from the most advanced among them, were to play a decisive part in the events of 1789. "It is those wretched priests who will be the end of us", said the Count of Antraigues at that time, and it was the clergy, indeed, who broke up the solidarity of the two privileged orders.

It was, therefore, not surprising that the clergy showed such anxiety to educate the people. In the country, the school-master, who was almost always cantor and sacristan as well, worked in close harmony with the parish priest. In the towns there were more and more houses of the Brothers of the Christian Schools, whose rule, dating from 1695, was revised in 1717. For the girls, St Louis Mary Grignon de Montfort founded the first establishment of the Sisters of La Sagesse at La Rochelle in 1715. A large number of local Congregations were founded during this century.

As regards grammar schools, it was still the Jesuits who had almost a monopoly in this respect, with colleges usually run as day schools. These gave instruction on very rigid lines, excessively dominated by the teaching of Latin, with very little practical work, but the masters who taught in them were highly-trained in pedagogy. There were some tentative efforts to get out of this groove, as, for instance, those of Charles Rollin (1661–1741), author of the *Traité des Etudes*, in which he attempted to reconcile the methods of the Jesuits and those of Port-Royal; and also of the Oratorians who opened the door slightly to the sciences.

It was not only the preponderance of Latin, but also the open scorn displayed for scientific studies, with a total dis-regard of the present, which could not fail to infuriate the Encyclopedists. This contributed to the campaigns which led finally to the suppression of the Jesuits. This action disorganized the whole of secondary education, and provided a good opportunity for putting it in the hands of the civil authority, a result duly effected by an edict of February, 1763. In reply to the protestations of the General Assembly of the Clergy, the Government replied that representatives of the Church would be consulted. What happened was that the military schools, such as Sorèze and Brienne, were entrusted to the religious, and it was the religious also who filled most of the vacancies left by the Jesuits, whose programmes and methods were largely followed, as parents and scholars had become used to them.

Although they were still important, advanced religious studies suffered from the doctrinal disputes, caused by Gallicanism and Jansenism, since these diverted the specialists from studies of permanent value, or gave a questionable bias to their works. Oratorians and Dominicans were thus contaminated by Jansenism. This century produced, however, some estimable works, such as the *Histoire de l'Église* by Claude Fleury, the biblical works of Dom Calmet, and the *Histoire générale des auteurs sacrés ecclésiastiques*, of Dom Ceillier, a masterly work in twenty-five volumes. France benefited from the *Recueil des historiens des Gaules et de la France* begun by Dom Bouquet; from the *Histoire littéraire de la France*, the first eight volumes of which were published by Dom Rivet; and from the *Histoire du Languedoc* by Dom Vaissette.

Apologists of the highest rank would have been required to meet the attacks of the Encyclopedists, the verve of Voltaire, or the utopian ideas of Rousseau. Not such were Père Nonnotte, nor Abbé Guénée, nor Le Franc de Pompignan, although the writings of the last named were very substantial. As for pulpit eloquence, even though this was not quite as extinct as has been stated, there was none which came

anywhere near the standard set up by the great preachers of
the seventeenth century, except for the preaching of Massillon,
who died in 1740. There was certainly a continuing missionary eloquence, upheld by St Grignon de Montfort in the
West and in the South by Père Bridaine, the latter being
extremely original.

The spiritual life of the eighteenth century suffered greatly
from Jansenism, but possibly even more so from the condemnation of Quietism, which turned many authors away from
mysticism and obliged them to exercise great prudence in
their writings. To those who assert that, long before Quietism
began, the mystical movement had, in any case, begun to show
signs of exhaustion, it can be argued that Quietism registered
precisely a new departure. Without having produced any outstanding work, religious thought revealed an ideal of gentleness and peace, often described with singular charm. Such
was the *Abandon à la Providence divine* of Fr de Caussade,
or the *Traité de la Paix intérieure* of de Lombez, or *Les
Caractères de la vraie dévotion* of N. Grou, or, again, the
writings of Fr de Clorivière. These books revealed havens of
peace existing in that age of intellectual dispute, and, fundamentally, how are we to know whether it is the best-known
characters who are the most representative of that century,
which is so badly known? The merciless banter of the philosophical writers, the sadistic pleasure of the onlookers at the
guillotine in the Place de Grève, and the monstrous egoism
of a mountebank vilifying a soul for a moment's pleasure,
all these are probably very little by comparison with the in-
nate goodness and the true charity of so great a number. One
is led to believe this is so, when so much intelligent generosity,
so much disinterestedness is found running through so many
records which cannot lie; offices for helping the poor, legal
aid, interest-free loans and that admirable institution, born
in the seventeenth century, to be sure, but remaining full of

life until well on in the eighteenth century, namely, the "common alms", instituted by Fr Chaurand, Christian mutual benefit in the confraternities. It is also worthy of note that the Spirit breathed its grace not only in the country cottage but also in the midst of the most opulent vice, and that St Benedict Labre was exactly contemporaneous with Louise de France, daughter of Louis XV and herself a Carmelite.

CHAPTER XVI

SEPARATED BRETHREN

In the previous chapter it was shown that it was possible to divide the eighteenth century in France into two distinctive periods, one being the years before 1760, when doctrinal disputes were dominant, and the other from 1760 to the Revolution of 1789, in which the influence of the philosophers was more conducive to a spirit of tolerance. However approximate these dates, and without emphasis on absolute synchronization, it can be stated that the enmity between religious denominations did diminish in a number of countries towards the middle of the century. The principle of *cujus regio ejus religio* was no longer in practice, and there was relative freedom, especially in Protestant countries.

In France, the first period had been a very hard time for the Protestants, and there was a general feeling that the Government did not wish to allow the results achieved by the Revocation of the Edict of Nantes to be prejudiced in any way. It was agreed, and indeed proclaimed officially in 1715, that there were no longer any Protestants in the country, and anything which gave the lie to this assertion was rigorously attacked. From the beginning of the Regency period, a shattering denial of this assertion was made by a revival and a reorganization of French Protestantism, of which the moving spirit was Pastor Antoine Court (1696–1760). The Huguenot Churches secretly convened again in the Cevennes, where services were held, known as "the secret assemblies", in precarious security, with sentinels posted to give warning of danger. Veritable networks were set up in other regions; their effectiveness was shown by the meeting of the synods in France itself. Nor could the results of their missionary work be denied; the centre of this movement was in Lausanne, at a seminary founded by Antoine Court out of reach of the French government. The administrators of the provinces took the most merciless action against them; pastors executed, faithful Protestants sent to the galleys or to prison, dragon-nades, all swelled the list of Protestant martyrs. Nevertheless, towards the middle of the century, the Protestant churches were reconstituted in Languedoc as well as in Dauphiny, Poitou and in the Massif Central. This was the time the last great persecution took place. As has been said, public opinion had changed, and a further attack, launched ten years later, was carried out without much enthusiasm, and produced little result. In their hearts, the Catholic clergy itself, in view of the advance of rationalism and agnosticism, could not view without compassion the sincerity of these Christian Huguenots. In the next few years, toleration made rapid strides, and not only could Protestants practise their religion without danger in Languedoc and Normandy, but legislative action was taken, in the years just before the Revolution, to restore to them their fundamental freedoms.

If the Huguenots preserved a remarkable unity, it was because nothing unites people like suffering for a common ideal. In more tolerant countries, on the contrary, various beliefs proliferated. This spectacle may give some pharisaical satisfaction to a Catholic, happy enough in being sure of his own faith, but, for one on the borderline of doubt, this diversity of belief is as moving as is the sight of a blind man gropingly feeling his way. With Pascal, it may be thought that to seek God is already to have found him and that there can be true sanctity on the borderline of faith. It is in this spirit that some of these sects will now be studied, since in a world where everything increasingly tends to hold together, they have not been without their influence even within the Church.

Thus Pietism continued to exercise a wide influence in the Germanic countries. The hostility it had encountered in the days of Spener had been forced to give way before the popularity of this beguiling spirituality. At the beginning of the century, its main centre had been in Saxony, especially at the new university of Halle, in connection with which the Pietists set up institutions for teaching and assistance. But the movement had adherents throughout Germany, particularly in Swabia, with Bengel, and in the Rhineland, where Gerhard Tersteegen wrote hymns which are amongst the most beautiful in the German tongue. The Pietists even organized missions to heathen countries, a most exceptional thing for Protestants to do at that period. But their weakness was that they could not always reconcile their rigorist ideas with the needs of life and, paradoxically, they allowed individual tendencies to develop, which gave rise to sects of dubious eccentricity.

Directly springing from Pietism, was the brotherhood founded at Herrnhut, in Lusatia, by Count von Zinzendorf (1700–1760). An admirer of Spener, he gathered together on a property he had there Moravian Brethren and persecuted Pietists, not without suffering persecution himself. This "fold of the Lord" (Herrnhut), a strange community of work and prayer, was able to continue in existence owing to the generosity and disarming purity of intention of its founder, in spite of its eccentricity, and it was even recognized by the Lutheran Church. Its members spread into England, America, and as far afield as the West Indies and Greenland. Today it still has 80,000 adherents.

Methodism can be said to have some relationship with Pietism. It originated from a group of students at Oxford, whom Charles Wesley gathered together, in about 1730, for prayer in common and the performance of good works. Teasing friends called them "the Holy Club", and later on, the *Methodists*, because of their regular religious exercises. Charles's elder brother, namely John Wesley (1704–91) soon became the active spirit of this small association and transformed it into a veritable religious movement. Having become an Anglican priest, he still retained his eclecticism, finding his inspiration in Catholic spiritual books as well as from his contacts with the Moravian Brothers and with Zinzendorf himself. In 1735, he was ably seconded by a powerful orator, George Whitefield, whose missions in England and in America had already proved highly successful. John Wesley himself, after having spent two years in America, and being enriched by his experiences, seeing the ineffectiveness of the Anglican clergy, already lacking zeal in their contacts with their people, began his journeys with his companions, all their preaching being done in the open air. After the first hesitations, due to the originality of his methods, had been overcome, he was very successful. The hostility of the Established Church, which refused to admit him into its churches, resulted in his having, of necessity, to follow his Method. He always considered himself to be a member of that Church, but he progressively became the leader of a dissident sect, going so far as to ordain his own ministers. Bearing in mind the atmosphere of scepticism and the moral crisis in English society circles at that time, as revealed in its literature or in the paintings of Hogarth, the work done by Wesley should not be underestimated. At the same time as he was bringing the people back to their faith, he was performing a great social duty by campaigning against alcoholism and debauchery, and by setting up homes, dispensaries, societies for lending money and, indeed, a whole network of philanthropic institutions. This movement came at a providential time, just at the time when England was beginning to be transformed into a great industrial nation, with all the human problems that such an evolution implies. British morale was renewed again, and it·can be said that Methodism achieved for Anglo-Saxon Protestantism and the English mentality itself, what Pietism brought to the Germanic world, but with still greater effectiveness on the part of the Methodists. From the middle of the century, the pace of this transformation increased, and, having found again a somewhat puritan strain, English people developed that reserve, those solid virtues and that altruism still to be found in the immense majority of them.

Methodism spread just as quickly in America, where Whitefield made a number of lengthy visits, as it did in Germany and Switzerland. Granted that this movement gave new life to Protestantism, beginning of course with Anglicanism, it could not escape separatist tendencies, of which the chief was that of organization with or without bishops.

The development which has just been described, gives an impression of a degree of freedom in violent contrast with the fate of the Russian Church. Although the Czar Peter the Great (1689–1725), can claim the merit of opening up Russia to Western influence and thus making it into a Great Power, his absolute rule could not allow of the existence of a patriarch in Moscow. He did away with that institution, and replaced it, in 1721, by a Holy Synod consisting of the bishops and Church functionaries designated by him, who met under the chairmanship of a procurator, a high lay officer. This was the beginning of a subordination of Church to State which was to last until 1917, being strengthened indeed by the free-thinking Catherine the Great (1762–96). It was in her reign that the partitions of Poland put profoundly Catholic peoples under what can well be termed the yoke of Russia. Despite the treaties which guaranteed freedom of religion to the two rites, the Latin and the Ruthenian, in communion with Rome, the most brutal and most underhand treatment was inflicted on them. A huge majority of the Uniates were forced to support a schism, and, if the Roman

Catholics were generally able to practise their religion, they felt the whole weight of the inflictions, not to say persecutions, which sought to reach, in their Catholicism, one of the essential elements of their national conscience.

For the Russian Church, this century was a time of constant degradation, which it is not proposed to describe here. It should be said, however, to what an extent, on the whole, the people clung to their faith. Though often of a primitive nature it was affecting in its charity. On this account, Russia remained Holy Russia with its real saints, hermits, pilgrims and monks. Some of them resolutely continued to live on the fringe of the official national Church and it was precisely the failures of that Church which gave rise to the formation of a great variety of sects, from the time of the Raskolniki in the middle of the seventeenth century. These sects showed many peculiarities to be sure, but very high ideals could still be found among them.

CHAPTER XVII

MISSIONARY WORK

If for the losses inflicted on the Church by the rise of indifference or unbelief compensation is sought in the conquests made in the heathen countries, it will only result in disappointment. The struggle went on, but the obstacles became greater, and powerful opposition arose. These obstacles were to be found in the very places from which the missionaries were recruited. Religious disputes and the new spirit had a disastrous effect on vocations. The question of the Chinese rites and a similar difficulty in Malabar, in which the Jesuits were opposed to other religious Orders, had deplorable results on the natives of those countries. After the condemnation by Rome of the heathen customs which the Jesuits considered could be preserved, conversions, in China at least, became very rare. In that country, the persecution which began again in the second quarter of the century, resulted in their drying up altogether. Finally, the suppression of the Society of Jesus, in which missionary work had been a traditional activity, completely disorganized the Churches founded in Asia and the New World. The other religious Orders were unable to take over this work with any success.

Hostility came primarily from the Protestant colonial powers, for instance, from England, whose domains had increased considerably during the century. That country did not willingly admit missionaries who were both foreign and Catholic and, in any case, it now had its own missionaries,

Methodists and others, as described earlier in this book. It came also from the United Provinces, to which the missionary idea was totally foreign and whose colonial system would not have accepted any effort to raise the status of the natives, on however small a scale. Opposition also came from an old Catholic country like Portugal, which now only retained the shreds of its former possessions in India, but still clung jealously to the rights given to it by the Holy See, and put obstacles in the way of the missionaries, although it was no longer able to provide them itself in anything like adequate numbers. It was Portugal, also, which was mainly responsible for the ruin of the missions in Paraguay, where missions had prospered until the middle of the eighteenth century. A boundary treaty with Spain in 1750 caused the displacement, by force, of thirty thousand Catholic Indians, who then revolted. By a piece of trickery, falsely imputed to the Jesuits in the campaign then being waged against them, they were held responsible for this revolt, and found themselves, in the colonies and in Portugal itself, subjected to persecution which went so far as the execution of a Jesuit Father, an old man, for heresy and high treason. One of the most disgraceful underhand features of this matter, was the influence of the rich importers of "black ivory" (slaves), who were opposed to the setting-up of "reductions", that is, native religious settlements.

In North America, it was France which had created the most lively Catholic communities up to the time of the loss of Canada and of Louisiana. Previous to that time however, the community of Acadia (Nova Scotia), had been forcibly transferred by the Treaty of Utrecht, and the English had shown great energy in hampering the missionary work of the clergy and in submerging the French inhabitants by an influx of British immigrants, with their centre in Halifax. In 1755, during the Seven Years War, this French community remained faithful enough to its home country to appear suspect to the

British authorities. It was at this time that there occurred the mass deportation, with its man hunts, a sinister forerunner of the mass displacements of our own times. The Acadians were scattered about in different parts of English America, but they retained their faith and their language, and many of them returned later to Nova Scotia, or settled to the East of the Great Lakes.

One of the results of the Treaty of Paris (1763) was that French religious Orders were prevented from continuing to help their brethren in America, even in Canada, while the novitiates of foreign communities were closed. The missions disappeared one after the other, or were abandoned, but the Canadian clergy remained on the banks of the St Lawrence to maintain the Catholic faith and French traditions.

This was in contrast with the thirteen English colonies in America, where Catholics were barely tolerated, even in Maryland, which had, indeed, been founded by a Catholic, its first parish of Baltimore dating from 1755. But the movement which was leading the Americans towards independence aroused great hopes in this small community. It inspired in John Carroll (1735–1815), a priest of Irish origin, the idea of enlisting his coreligionists in this struggle, and he was one of those who, after victory had been won, succeeded in getting freedom of conscience inscribed in the Constitution. Pius VI, taking advantage of the position thus created, made Carroll head of the missions in the United States, and he shortly became the first bishop of the new Republic. It soon fell to him to welcome the priests expelled from France by the Revolution of 1789, many of whom, after a fruitful ministry abroad, became illustrious as clergy or even as bishops under the Concordat in France.

As for Africa, results there were so indifferent, in spite of great devotion, that to attempt to give even a short account of them would falsify their real value by comparison with the scale of this book. For those who may be surprised at the contrast between these early results and the missionary developments in the nineteenth century, it should be pointed out that lack of means does not explain everything. It was not just by chance that the abolition of slavery coincided with the rapid progress of the missions, nor was it just by chance that Christianity penetrated into the interior of that continent by the same road as colonization, and not mere random trading, and led to the implantation there of European civilization. These may only be obvious facts, but there are certain obvious facts which must, in all good faith, be mentioned.

CONCLUSION

This book takes this history only as far as the eve of the French Revolution of 1789, forerunner of so many others, for this date is the real end of the eighteenth century. The ensuing years were to be some of the most agonizing the Church has ever known. It was not only that crowns were falling but that churches were being closed, as if the King of Heaven were to be held responsible for the errors or the weakness of the kings of the earth, and as if liberty, equality and fraternity, then proclaimed as something new, were not the essence of the doctrine of the Church, forgotten even by those who professed to practise it. The inventory made in this book of errors, frailties and omissions, is far from exhaustive. Monarchs, abusing their powers, have compromised the Church, just as churchmen have themselves distorted its message. An important result of the Revolution has been the liberation of the Church from the bonds which forced it to temporize with absolute power and privilege. It was thus enabled to gain far more in moral authority than it lost in temporal power. The subsequent religious revival does not actually fall within the scope of this book, but two remarks should be made which are apposite in this context.

The first, which is in line with what has been said above, is that Christianity should not be regarded as being systematically opposed to the philosophical movement. Philosophers bitterly opposed Christianity and Christians regarded philosophers as the worst enemies of their doctrine. On both sides, there were impassioned supporters and sectarians, but it is very rarely that men, who after all are not just brutes, do evil for evil's sake. What was lacking was the ability to see absolutely clearly, and also to free themselves from their prejudices. This having been said, a Christian cannot deny all sympathy to those who sought an ideal of humanity and justice outside a deformed Church. Looking back, on a final analysis we can see that they too worked for the ultimate good of the Church.

Secondly, it must be said that the gap between the two centuries reviewed here and the nineteenth century, is not as wide as may generally be supposed. Since the Revolution marked the end of many things and the beginning of many others, the extent to which it has been studied, in France and elsewhere, is out of proportion with its duration, for after all, it lasted for comparatively few years. It would, therefore, be a great mistake to think that men were entirely different after the Revolution, and that they formed a new generation. During the Revolution, and under the Empire and the Restoration, fully mature people held public office, certainly with young people too. But those older men had received all their training under the *ancien régime*. It has been pointed out that, among the bishops who revived the Church in France after the Concordat and also under Charles X, some of the most important of them had taken orders under Louis XV. In many cases they carried through a programme which they had drawn up in their early years but which there had been no opportunity of putting into practice at an earlier date. How many were the reforms which had been planned but never carried out and how many were the disasters which would have been avoided if those planned reforms had been accomplished!

The two centuries covered in this review are especially important in this general study, because the seventeenth century was a great century in its own right, while it was in the eighteenth century that the great days of the following years were hammered into shape.

SELECT BIBLIOGRAPHY

In this series: COGNET, Louis: *Post-Reformation Spirituality*; DE VAULX, Bernard: *History of the Missions*; KRANZ, Gisbert: *Modern Christian Literature* (British edn, Three Centuries of Christian Literature); WOODRUFF, Douglas: *Church and State*.

ATTWATER, Donald: *Martyrs: From St Stephen to John Tung*, London and New York, Sheed and Ward, 1952.

BEDOYÉRE, M. de la: *The Archbishop and the Lady: the Story of Fénelon and Mme Guyon*, London, Collins, 1956.

CALVET, Jean: *St Vincent de Paul*, translated by Lancelot C. Sheppard, London, Burns and Oates, and New York, David McKay, 1952.

DANIEL-ROPS, Henri: *Monsieur Vincent: The Story of St Vincent de Paul*, New York, Hawthorn Books, 1961.

FRANCIS DE SALES, St: *Introduction to the Devout Life*, translated by Michael Day, London, Burns and Oates, and Westminster, Md, Newman Press, 1956; *Selected Letters*, translated with an Introduction by Elizabeth Stopp, London, Faber, 1960.

HAMON, M.: *Life of St Francis of Sales*, London, Burns and Oates, 1925.

HAZARD, Paul: *The European Mind (1680–1715)*, London, Hollis and Carter, and New Haven, Conn., Yale Univ. Press, 1953; *European Thought in the Eighteenth Century*, London, Hollis and Carter, and New Haven, Conn., Yale Univ. Press, 1954.

HUGHES, P.: *A History of the Catholic Church*, three volumes, London and New York, Sheed and Ward, 1934–47; *A Popular History of the Catholic Church*, London, Burns and Oates, and New York, Macmillan, 1939 (reprint, 1958).

KENTON, Edna: *Black Gowns and Redskins* (Jesuit missionaries in North America, 1610–1791), London, Longmans, and New York, Vanguard, 1959; *Jesuit Relations*, New York, Vanguard, 1953.

KNOX, R. A.: *Enthusiasm, a Chapter in the History of Religion with special Reference to the Seventeenth and Eighteenth Centuries*, London and New York, Oxford Univ. Press, 1950.

LATOURETTE, K. S.: *History of the Expansion of Christianity*, seven volumes, London, Eyre and Spottiswoode, and New York, Harper, 1939–45.

LEYS, M. D. R.: *Catholics in England, 1559–1829, A social history*, London and New York, Longmans, 1961.

PASTOR, Ludwig von: *The History of the Popes from the Close of the Middle Ages*, forty volumes, London, Kegan Paul, and St Louis, Herder, 1937–50.

POURRAT, Pierre: *Christian Spirituality*, volumes I–III, London, Burns and Oates, 1922–4; volumes I–IV, Westminster, Md, Newman Press, 1953–8.

SHEPPARD, Lancelot C.: *Barbe Acarie, Wife and Mystic*, London, Burns and Oates, and New York, David McKay, 1953.

WATKIN, E. I.: *Roman Catholicism in England from the Reformation to 1950*, London and New York, Oxford Univ. Press, 1957.

The Twentieth Century
Encyclopedia of Catholicism

The number of each volume indicates its place in the over-all series and not the order of publication.

PART ONE: KNOWLEDGE AND FAITH

PART TWO: THE BASIC TRUTHS

All titles are subject to change.